DVMS Institute®

Thriving on the Edge of Chaos

David Moskowitz
David M. Nichols

A holistic approach to organizational cyber-resilience

tso
a Williams Lea company

tso
a Williams Lea company

Published by TSO (The Stationery Office), part of Williams Lea,
www.tsoshop.co.uk

Mail, Telephone, Fax & Email
TSO
PO Box 29, Norwich, NR3 1GN
Telephone orders/General enquiries: 0333 202 5070
Fax orders: 0333 202 5080
Email: customer.services@tso.co.uk
Textphone 0333 202 5077
www.tsoshop.co.uk

DVMS Institute LLC
742 Mink Ave., #135
Murrells Inlet, SC 29576
Phone (401) 764-0721
www.dvmsinstitute.com

Authors: David Moskowitz and David M. Nichols

Subject Matter Expert and Chief Examiner: David Moskowitz

If you have any feedback that you would like to record in our change control log, please send this to **commissioning@williamslea.com**

Print 9780117094741
PDF 9780117094833
ePub 9780117094840

Contents

Foreword

The digital landscape is evolving faster than ever before, bringing new challenges for cybersecurity professionals. This increasing complexity and unpredictability – a state often described as volatile, uncertain, complex, and ambiguous (VUCA) – means that organizations now face unprecedented problems and multi-faceted threats. Strategic adaptability and human-centered decision-making are crucial for success.

With their vast wealth of knowledge and hands-on experience, the authors of *Thriving on the Edge of Chaos* emphasize a holistic approach to cybersecurity as an aspect of resiliency, offering a perspective that goes beyond its technical aspects. Central to this approach is the concept that treats their Digital Value Management System® as an overlay – a framework developed to bridge the gap between technology and human psychology, helping readers understand the intersections of complexity thinking, change management, and systems thinking within the digital realm. This approach is not theoretical; it offers actionable strategies and guidance for those who navigate the constantly shifting cybersecurity landscape.

The overlay views the security ecosystem as a complex, dynamic network of interconnected parts, where small changes in one area may trigger unexpected impacts across the system. This perspective encourages professionals to anticipate and prepare for interactions with threats, vulnerabilities, and defenses in non-linear ways, enabling them to adapt swiftly to unforeseen challenges. Systems thinking principles play a significant part in the overlay, offering a structured approach to managing the complexities, focusing on the design, analysis, and optimization of each component of the organizational environment. The principles of change management also play a critical role within the overlay, ensuring that cybersecurity practices evolve with the organization and that all stakeholders successfully adopt new processes, technologies, and behaviors. Collectively, these disciplines promote a comprehensive approach that empowers all professionals to respond to and shape their complex environments with agility and foresight.

Thriving on the Edge of Chaos provides readers with both valuable insights and practical advice, equipping them to not only understand the complexities of modern cybersecurity but to thrive within it actively. This book is an essential read for anyone seeking to turn the VUCA world of cybersecurity from a source of stress and uncertainty into an opportunity for growth and resilience.

Rebecca McKeown, *Chartered Psychologist, founder of Mind Science Ltd, and visiting fellow at Cranfield University*

Preface

When we wrote *Fundamentals of Adopting the NIST Cybersecurity Framework* and *A Practitioner's Guide to Adapting the NIST Cybersecurity Framework*, we recognized that the concepts presented in those publications had broader implications beyond cybersecurity and technology.

Although we did not explicitly state it, we believed that cybersecurity should not be seen as a goal but rather as a byproduct of a comprehensive approach to organizational resilience. While cybersecurity is essential, the principles of effective and adaptable governance – ranging from the boardroom to the break room – depend on the understanding that cybersecurity cannot and will never be a preventative measure; it's a delay tactic that recognizes the difference between "when" versus "if" there will be a cyber-breach. Therefore, the ultimate goal should be organizational resilience, defined as the ability to recover from or adapt to adversity or change. Resilience, in this sense, is broader than cybersecurity, encompassing natural disasters, war, pandemics, and more. It is the organizational ability to maintain or rapidly restore operations during any of these events (including a cyber-attack).

Our previous work highlighted the importance of senior leadership in driving cybersecurity initiatives. Leadership must actively promote a culture of continual learning and adaptation. The most resilient organizations do not just endure crises but turn challenges into opportunities for growth. This guide invites leaders and practitioners to explore how strategic foresight, cultural agility, and a commitment to learning can create the foundation for a truly resilient organization.

At the heart of this publication is a call to rethink the fundamental assumptions that underpin our organizational structures and behaviors. By examining mental models, leadership practices, and the principles of a learning organization, we can uncover new pathways to resilience. This holistic approach draws inspiration from the works of thought leaders and pioneers in the field. We explore how to apply leverage to the system that is the organization, enabling continual innovation and sustainable growth.

Thriving on the Edge of Chaos is structured around seven minimum viable capabilities that every organization must master: Govern, Assure, Plan, Design, Change, Execute, and Innovate. Everything the organization already does falls into one or more of these capabilities that provide a comprehensive framework for understanding and enhancing the intricate web of relationships within your organization and the ecosystem in which it exists. In other words, what we propose is not a new framework or method but an overlay – which is the way we designed the Digital Value Management System®. It's not a one-size-fits-all; it's an adaptable-by-all.

Incorporating the insights and experiences from various industries, our goal was to provide a comprehensive approach to building resilient organizations. We delve into the critical aspects of organizational culture, leadership, and learning, offering practical strategies and tools to help organizations navigate the complexities of the modern business landscape. By embracing the principles outlined in this guide, organizations can better prepare for the unexpected and turn challenges into opportunities for growth and transformation.

As you embark on this journey, we invite you to reflect on how your organization responds to change and adversity. Consider how the ideas expressed can be applied to your unique context. Embrace the idea that resilience is not a destination but an ongoing process of learning, adaptation, and innovation. Together, we can build organizations that withstand the test of time and thrive.

David Moskowitz, *Executive Director for Content Development, DVMS Institute LLC*

David Nichols, *Executive Director, DVMS Institute LLC*

About the authors

David Moskowitz

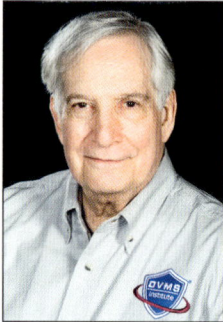

David is the content architect of the DVMS Institute. In this role, he actively looks for and works with subject matter experts to develop relevant content for the institute.

David started his formal career as an operating systems programmer and systems architect, before going on to look at different forms of systems and complexity while serving in the US Army. After his military service, he continued to apply a systems approach to his job, working on an anti-submarine warfare program for the US Department of Defense. By applying a whole-systems perspective, he addressed organizational and inter-personal issues and created a high-performing team.

The team stumbled into an approach that today many people would recognize as parts of IT service management and Kanban. It included a formalized approach to managing change, combined with incremental development performed in short iterations that received constant feedback. Later, as a consultant, he assisted organizations in adopting what they considered to be technical disruptions, applying a critical lesson learned from experience: "Every problem was, at its core, a people problem, not a technology problem." Technology was either an enabler or an inhibitor. The recurring mantra of these efforts was, "Solve the problem; don't treat the symptom."

David first met Dave Nichols in 2008, and since then they have worked together to develop a systems approach to accelerate the creation and delivery of business value. David views cybersecurity as a critical aspect of quality and value.

David thanks his wife Rosemary for her patience, tolerance and encouragement, without whom this book would not have been possible. He can be contacted at david.moskowitz@dvmsinstitute.com; for more information, visit www.dvmsinstitute.com.

David Nichols

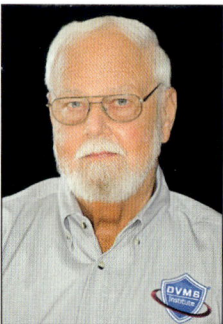

Dave is the executive director of the DVMS Institute. The institute's mission is to enable organizations to create, protect, and deliver digital business value through a curated portfolio of content and programs that bring value to its member stakeholders. Dave's role is to work with the industry's leading practitioners in risk management, service management, cybersecurity, assurance, and business leadership to produce industry-leading guidance and programs that will enable organizations to survive and thrive in a digital business world.

Dave spent his formative years on US Navy submarines, where he gained his knowledge of complex systems and how to function in high-performance teams. He took these skills into civilian life, where he built a successful career in software development and service delivery.

In 2000, Dave formed itSM Solutions with his partners, Janet Kuhn and Rick Lemieux, to create and deliver service management certification training and consulting programs to Fortune 500 companies. In 2015, his team created the award-winning APMG-accredited NIST Cybersecurity Framework training scheme, which teaches organizations how to rapidly engineer and operationalize a cybersecurity risk management program.

Dave would like to thank Zelda, his wife of more than 50 years, for her support and inspiration when it was needed most. He can be contacted at david.nichols@dvmsinstitute.com; for more information, visit www.dvmsinstitute.com.

Acknowledgments

DVMS Institute and TSO kindly thank those who participated in the production of this title:

Roy Atkinson, Clifton Butterfield, LLC

Michael Battistella, Solutions³ LLC

Jacob Hill, GRC Academy

Bradley Laatsch, Hewlett-Packard Enterprise

Mike Longarzo, formerly Solutions³ LLC

Rebecca McKeown, Chartered Psychologist, Mind Science

Amy McLaughlin, Oregon State University

Ed Moses, Specialist Industries Ltd

Kristen Nova, Solutions³ LLC

Dr. Douglas Rose, American Public University System

Patrick von Schlag, Deep Creek Center

LJ 'Butch' Sheets, Service Management Dynamix LLC

Roger Theriault, retired IT consultant

J Price Williams, Iram Consulting Ltd

DVMS Institute would also like to thank the team at TSO for their collaborative efforts in coordinating and improving the material.

This book was 12 years in the making. We dedicate it to Rick Lemieux, our patient and unwavering cheerleader.

CHAPTER 1
Thriving on the edge

1 Thriving on the edge

"If you change the way you look at things, the things you look at change."
Dr. Wayne Dyer

Imagine gazing into a swirling maelstrom, where chaos reigns and hidden dangers lurk beneath the surface. This is the reality of the digital landscape, a sea of endless opportunity riddled with treacherous currents and unpredictable storms. Organizations navigating these waters face an ever-present question: Will they succumb to the perils, or can they forge a path toward resilience?

Consider the quotation from Wayne Dyer above. What does it mean to change how you look at things? Changing how we look at things requires changing how we think – reframing what we see and experience by changing our assumptions and "reconceptualizing" the problem we face. What happens if we apply this wisdom to the digital landscape? What if we reframe it as an opportunity instead of focusing on the storm? This is the transformative power of the Digital Value Management System® (DVMS).

The DVMS is neither a framework nor a method: it is an overlay that acts like a lens through which an organization can gain a new perspective on digital risk, revealing gaps and empowering proactive strategies. It's not a one-size-fits-all solution but an adaptable and scalable guide for organizations of any size, from agile startups to established giants.

1.1 Thinking differently

At the heart of the power of the DVMS are the people within the organization who are learning to see and think in systems as part of what it does to thrive. However, the results will be short-term without a holistic approach that encompasses organizational leadership, accountability, and culture.

What's needed is a different perspective. While there is some disagreement over the origin of the sage advice that "insanity is doing the same thing over and over again and expecting different results," there is no doubt that Albert Einstein put it most succinctly: "We can't solve problems by using the same kind of thinking we used when we created them."

This systematic approach is anchored in the seven core capabilities of the DVMS: Govern, Assure, Plan, Design, Change, Execute, and Innovate (called the "minimum viable capabilities" ["MVC"] in the text of this book). These capabilities encompass the entire organization, from strategic planning and risk management to project execution and continual improvement. Mapping existing practices to these core areas enables an organization to identify performance gaps and build a comprehensive system for managing digital business risk.

1.2 Using this book

To make this journey easier, we've created several models and approaches to facilitate thinking and seeing differently. Some sections might be obvious, requiring only a quick read to "get the idea." However, other parts of the book may require more thought and contemplation.

Chapter 2 establishes the DVMS foundation that seamlessly integrates strategy-risk and the MVC. By establishing a clear risk appetite and robust approach to governance, the DVMS empowers leaders to make informed decisions, balancing ambition with calculated risk-taking. Because the DVMS is an overlay, it is independent of and unbiased toward frameworks, methods, or standards. The justification for treating the DVMS as an overlay is based on the idea that every organization exists within a complex ecosystem – making the organization a part of a complex adaptive system (CAS). The chapter introduces the CPD Model to explain the nature of an overlay to the organizational system. As you'll see in the chapter, every organization enters the model at the same place, at the point in the model labeled "Adapt."

Another essential idea introduced in Chapter 2, and repeated throughout the book, is the significant role that culture plays in organizational success. Although some may perceive culture as a vague or ambiguous notion, we recommend considering organizational culture to be an aspect of strategy-risk; culture is either an enabler or an impediment to organizational resiliency.

Chapter 3 provides an approach to thinking differently by exploring the DVMS as an overlay, and the ramifications of taking this approach. It delves into mental models, leadership, and the imperative to curate a learning culture, something that doesn't happen overnight. It takes a 24×7×365 commitment for leaders to model the expected behaviors they want from others.

As an overlay, the DVMS encompasses what organizations already do. The chapter provides more specifics, briefly summarized here. The top layer of the overlay is what the organization already does; the middle layer is represented graphically as the DVMS Z-X Model, a visualization of how the MVC fits together – everything the organization does maps to one or more of these capabilities. The bottom layer operationalizes the middle layer: the DVMS Create, Protect, and Deliver Digital Business Value Model, or CPD Model for short.

The journey to achieve the capability to create and deliver appropriately protected digital business value requires a fundamental shift in perspective – seeing and thinking differently. Organizations must evolve from siloed approaches to embrace complexity as a reality, not an obstacle. This necessitates continual risk identification, assessment, and mitigation, fostering a culture where risk awareness permeates every decision.

This idea requires a different question: How does "this" affect "that"? We address these ideas in **Chapter 4**. As noted above in the description of Chapter 2, the role of culture is a repeated theme throughout this book. Chapter 3 introduced the idea of mental models and their relationship to organizational structure and behavior. Chapter 4 covers the relationship between leadership, accountability, and culture.

Chapter 5 builds on the information presented in the previous chapters and addresses what it takes to shape outcomes, by providing more details about the minimum viable capabilities, representing an ability to do something to create and deliver appropriately protected digital value. Each capability aggregates practice areas, which are collections of related practices that define outcomes. As noted in the chapter, practices define outcomes; it is an organizational responsibility to determine the activities, processes, and tasks that produce these outcomes.

Chapter 6 describes what it takes to build the team that will spearhead the adoption of the paradigm suggested by the DVMS. The chapter also introduces the idea of Praxis: a practical approach to turn theory into practice.

Chapter 7 extends the ideas, focusing on decisions and outcomes and what it takes to build a learning organization. This requires time and commitment that may require the organization to think differently – potentially radically so – starting with cultural changes to make "learning" sticky.

Chapter 8 summarizes the book with the idea that this is not the end: it's the beginning.

Throughout the book, we reinforce the idea that policy and culture cascade from the very top of the organization through every management layer to every person. It starts with the board of directors[1] (or similar entity) setting the strategic direction and holding leaders accountable. Leaders cultivate transparency, build trust, and communicate effectively across all levels, making them accountable for fostering a risk-aware and learning culture.

This approach allows an organization to define and achieve different outcomes, improve customer retention, and be resilient when facing challenges (e.g., the marketplace or the threat landscape). By integrating risk-informed decision-making into the portfolio, program, and project management through a Praxis approach, potential pitfalls are identified and addressed proactively. We advocate and emphasize practical application, learning from experience, and continually refining processes. As a caveat, while these approaches might seem simple, we don't want to suggest that they are easy. The psychology of learning to see and think differently requires building new mental models to reframe experiences – this takes practice and a long-term commitment.

1.3   The rest of the story

Our journey doesn't end here. Organizations must recognize the ever-evolving digital landscape and establish an ongoing and evolving "new normal." This entails working *on* and *in* the system, continually adapting the DVMS as an overlay to changing circumstances. Cultivating a learning organization fueled by a thirst for knowledge and data-driven insights becomes pivotal for sustainable success.

This book introduces the DVMS and the MVC concepts, and is key to understanding how to "see differently" and "think differently." It is based on the central idea that digital value created without appropriate protection has no sustainable value. This concept makes it essential for organizations to rethink how they develop and deliver value, from creating *then* protecting as serial events to creating *and* protecting as concurrent activities. To clarify this concept, an organization with a quality assurance department, or one that tests after completing development, operates in "create then protect" mode.

Creating and protecting digital business value requires a different approach that is risk-informed. It requires thinking about strategy and risk not as separate and distinct ideas but as a single entity that we call "strategy-risk," which becomes a pervasive factor in decision-making.

Are you ready to hold a lens to your organization and begin to think differently? Are you prepared to transform risk into resilience and unlock the true potential of your digital journey? Dive into this guide and discover how to use the DVMS as your compass, navigating you through the digital storm toward a future of sustainable success.

1.4   Chapter takeaways

Our goal for this book is to provide a 21st-century approach to business that changes the focus from "create *then* protect" to "create *and* protect" – as concurrent activities.

---

[1]   Throughout this book we use the term "board of directors" generically to apply to a governing body, steering committee or individual who owns the ultimate accountability and responsibility to organizational stakeholders.

CHAPTER 2

The Digital Value
Management System®

2 The Digital Value Management System®

Organizations face many challenges in an ever-changing digital landscape, stemming from complexity and digital business risk. They need a holistic and adaptive approach to navigate this intricate terrain and succeed in the digital age. The DVMS provides a systems-based overlay that facilitates managing organizational complexity and accounts for organizational culture as a vital component of success.

What does it mean to take a "systems-based" approach? To explain this idea, we start with something most people understand: an automobile. A car, like a business, is made up of many systems:

- Body and chassis – providing structural scaffolding for the other systems, including space for people and storage
- Engine (including cooling and lubrication)
- Fuel system
- Electrical system
- Drive train
- Brake system
- Steering
- Suspension
- Passenger environment
- Visibility (windshield wipers and washers, defrosting).

None of these individual systems provide transportation from point to point. We can drive the vehicle only when these appropriately designed and matching systems are combined, interconnected, and operating as a cohesive whole.

Similarly, any organization includes various systems, even if they aren't obvious. A one-person company must deal with customers, suppliers, regulatory and compliance issues, and more – requiring a minimal record-keeping system if nothing else. A systems-based approach aims to recognize these systems and work to avoid the silos that occur in many organizations. This idea regarding "desiloization," or making the organization operate with fewer silos, provides an approach that increases transparency between different parts of the enterprise.

This idea represents the essence of applying the DVMS to any organization; it is a systems-based approach that considers the whole of the organization (like the whole of the car) as a system of systems with a purpose.

Think about this for a moment.

The structure and behavior of the systems are inextricably linked. A Formula 1 racecar is still a car. However, it has a very different structure and behavior than the average car in everyday use. If you want better performance (behavior) from this average car, you must do something about its structure (e.g., better suspension, tires, balancing and tuning the engine).

The same thing is true for an organization – if you want different outcomes, you must address organizational structure and behavior.

The behaviors that occur within an organization express its culture (its worldview). The link between structure and behavior means that changing organizational culture will typically require making structural changes to the organization (e.g., reducing the layers of management).

The DVMS recognizes organizational culture as a central component of success. Culture shapes the collective mindset, values, and behavior, profoundly influencing how full- and part-time staff respond to challenges and opportunities. Fostering a culture that values experimentation, collaboration, and continual learning is paramount. The DVMS emphasizes aligning culture with core principles to create an environment that embraces change, enabling organizations to *Thrive on the Edge of Chaos*.

There is a caveat: Changing organizational culture is like trying to change the course and speed of a supertanker. Newton's laws of motion[2] apply in both cases. You can apply the "correction," but you must be patient before the results are fully and completely evident, because the organization (ship) has a lot of inertia that prevents instantaneous change.

This idea of "latency" inherent in working to change or adapt organizational culture is also an essential aspect of systems thinking. For now, here's a one-sentence definition for this term that we'll expand on in Chapter 3: "Systems thinking helps us understand complex situations by examining how different parts of a system interact and influence each other."

Applying leverage to a system (for example, applying it to change the course of our supertanker) doesn't immediately establish the new direction for the ship: it takes time for something that big to align with the new course heading. The same thing is true with organizations.

The DVMS is a system that overlays what the organization is already doing. It doesn't matter what standards, frameworks, methods, or approaches are already in place. The overlay covers everything the organization does (or plans to do).

The concept of the DVMS as an overlay is essential. The DVMS is scalable; the overlay approach potentially changes how an organization treats value creation and protection from serial to concurrent endeavors. Instead of separate ideas, the overlay treats the ideas as aspects of quality, regardless of size, encompassing everything the organization does, including cultural changes, digital trust, privacy, regulatory and compliance issues, and so on.

The DVMS is neither a framework nor a method. Frameworks are descriptive: they describe what to do, not how to do it. Methods provide guidelines to accomplish something without necessarily providing a way to adopt or adapt them. Frameworks and methods don't always easily scale – or at least don't provide an approach to scalability other than adapting or tailoring.

The difference between a framework or method and the DVMS is simple: the DVMS is not a one-size-fits-all – as an overlay, it's adaptable by all, regardless of size, by overlaying it on whatever frameworks and methods the organization already has or uses to expose performance gaps. We'll get into the details later in this chapter.

Making the DVMS truly scalable requires understanding several aspects. First, we created a set of seven MVC shared by all organizations. Every organization exhibits some form of the following capabilities arranged in what we call the DVMS Z-X Model (see Figure 2.1):

- **Govern** Provides appropriate governance that forms the basis for the organizational rules: "How we conduct business." It establishes the policies that define boundaries and scope, providing clear direction, values, and risk parameters, and ensuring alignment and responsible action. This extends to the policy cascade from strategic intent through management and execution to deliver the operational intent

- **Assure** Provides appropriate assurance that the organization does the right things the right way (e.g., conformance to the governance policies and within defined tolerances). This builds trust and confidence by fostering a culture of accountability to monitor and optimize performance and capabilities

---

2   Sir Isaac Newton postulated three laws of motion: (1) An object in a state of uniform motion (including at rest, which is zero motion) remains in motion until an outside force acts on it; (2) The acceleration of an object depends on the mass of the object and the amount of force applied (this is the classic $F = ma$ and implies the first law, i.e., zero acceleration means zero force applied); and (3) For every action there is an equal and opposite reaction (conservation of momentum – this follows from the second law).

- **Plan** Represents the planning effort that enables the organization to develop appropriate governance and assurance of these core capabilities – the policies describing what to do, and the associated approach to monitor and measure outcomes. It charts the course by crafting agile and responsive strategies to adapt to unforeseen changes and opportunities

- **Design** Enables the organization to create a cohesive approach to creating, protecting, and delivering digital business value – how to do it with the available resources, etc. It fosters an approach to experimentation with innovative solutions, focusing on creating, protecting, and delivering value

- **Change** Enables the organization to adapt to its environment. It enables the organization to embrace transformation by empowering individuals and teams to iterate, learn, and evolve in response to feedback and emerging needs

- **Execute** Represents the practice areas that create, protect, and deliver digital business value. Delivers the created and appropriately protected excellence by efficiently and effectively putting plans into action, optimizing the steps from ideation to realization

- **Innovate** Seeks opportunities to improve the creation, protection, and delivery of digital business value. It involves continually pushing boundaries by fostering a culture of curiosity and experimentation, seeking new ways to create, protect, and deliver value.

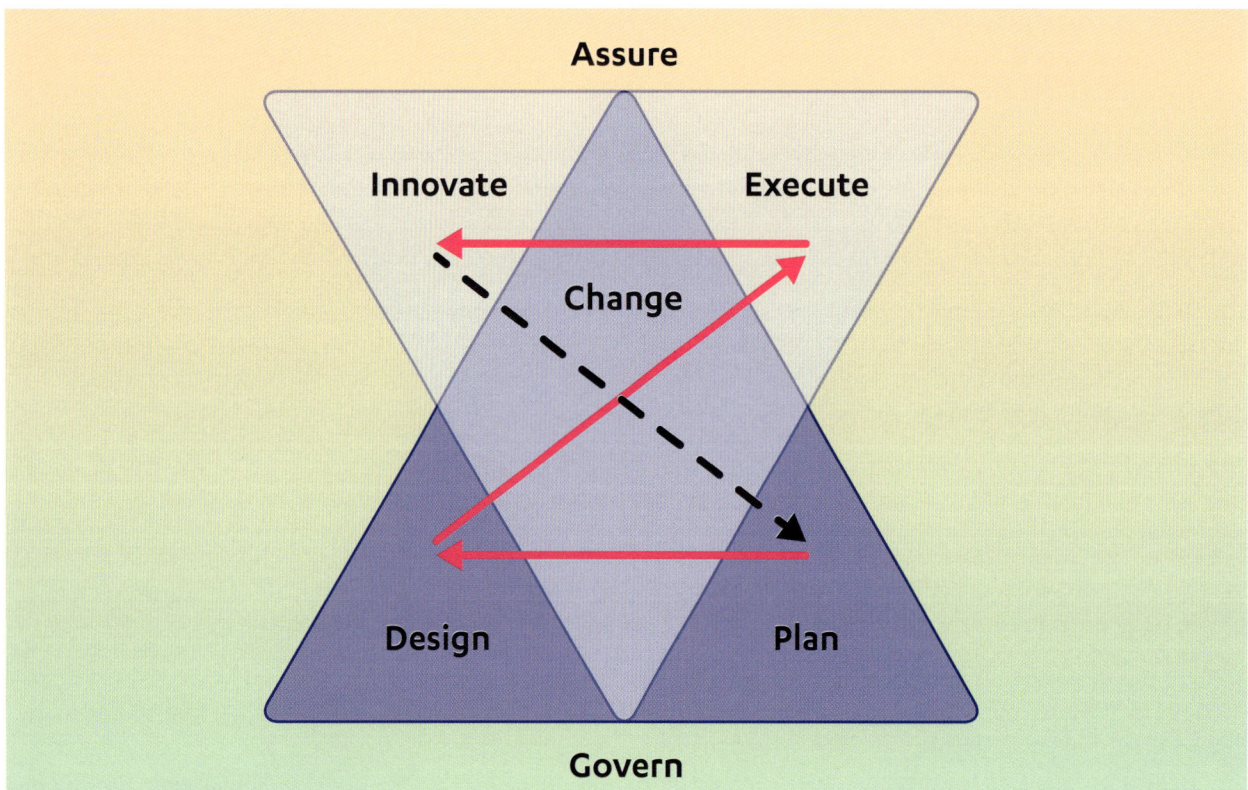

Figure 2.1 The DVMS Z-X Model

While most of the Z-X Model capabilities are relatively self-explanatory, the Innovate capability needs a brief expansion. We define four aspects of innovation:

- **Incremental** innovations are the small things every organization does to keep things running. In software development, these would typically be part of a point release (e.g., version 3.1 to 3.2)

- **Sustaining** innovations are more encompassing, introducing new features and benefits. Continuing the software analogy, these are major versions (e.g., 3.2 to 4.0)

- **Adaptive** innovations change policy
- **Disruptive** innovations result in strategic change.

Another way to achieve scalability is to work in phases that constitute what we call the DVMS FastTrack™ approach. If you're familiar with any agile method or approach, you'll recognize the origins of this approach. We recommend making small incremental and iterative adaptations organized into four phases:

- **Phase 0: Initiate** "Getting ready to get ready" establishes the baseline for subsequent phases – which may require implementing early-stage controls and maturing specific capabilities
- **Phase 1: Basic hygiene** Stabilize the environment
- **Phase 2: Expand** Optimize the environment
- **Phase 3: Innovate** Continual innovation from a stable and optimized state.

The phases do not represent a linear progression. Some things are ongoing in every phase (e.g., governance, assurance, program and project management, and risk assessment). An innovation in Phase 1 might impact aspects and outcomes in Phase 0, and so on.

Let's examine these ideas in more detail, starting with systems.

2.1 Structure and behavior

Before diving into the idea of structure and behavior, we need a bit of background that starts with the following set of core principles:

- **Customers drive value** There is a context to value that includes the following:

  - **Perception** A customer's (stakeholder's) point of view determines the value
  - **Protection** Efforts to protect value must be proportional to this perceived value
  - **Maintainability** The perception of value changes over time. Value to the customer (stakeholder) must be maintained in a dynamic and rapidly changing environment

- **Change is a constant** Every organization exists within a dynamic environment and must adapt its performance as needed. This concept might lead to changing everything (people, practice, technology, and structure) to maintain value delivery.

  Don't try to do everything simultaneously; work in phases – prioritize and approach change iteratively and in small increments. This approach supports experimentation; if a small increment doesn't work, you can recognize it sooner and make "iterative" adjustments sooner

- **Organizations are complex adaptive systems** This principle suggests that people adopt and apply systems thinking. Learning to think in systems requires understanding that a system is a collection of interrelated, interconnected, and interacting parts organized to accomplish a purpose. In simple terms, a system is a "whole" that consists of parts with the following characteristics:

  - Each part affects the behavior or properties of the whole
  - Each part of the system depends on the effect of some other part (or parts)
  - No part (or collection of parts) of the system has an independent effect
  - In other words, a system is not the sum of its parts but the product of their interactions
  - The perspective of the system depends on the view of the system, which in some cases might be limited to a few simple subsystems of the whole

- **Risk is an intrinsic aspect of strategy** No plan is perfect; no strategy is either. Every strategy includes aspects of uncertainty and risk. The DVMS incorporates a risk-informed approach to strategy called "strategy-risk."

Let's spend a few paragraphs focusing on the third principle: "Organizations are complex adaptive systems." Adopting and applying systems thinking supports understanding organizational complexities from multiple perspectives. We've already mentioned that the structure of a system is inextricably linked to the behavior of (and within) the system. Systems are dynamic. System behaviors (interactions) occur within a structure. A bouncing ball in a transparent box represents a relatively simple system. The behavior of the ball depends on the environmental structure (e.g., the "hardness" of the bounce surfaces, the type of ball [e.g., a soft rubber ball or a golf ball], air friction, temperature).

As the number of interactions increases and the structure changes, the system is no longer simple (e.g., imagine 100 balls dropping into the box and trying to track them all visually). Now, we have a complex system. It's not hard to imagine that as the balls bounce around the box, several of them will bump into each other, altering their speed and trajectory, making visual tracking even more difficult. The system of bouncing balls changed as they collided with each other. This system adapts to changes. As the balls bounce and bump into each other, the structure changes (e.g., the balls don't bounce as high, balls that bounce into each other change direction).

Suppose we change the structure of the box (e.g., make it smaller, make the walls harder or softer): the bouncing and colliding behavior of the balls will also change. To recast this in organizational terms, altering the structural aspects of the organization (e.g., management levels, reporting rigor) impacts the resulting behavior of the people affected by the change.

2.1.1 Considering systems thinking: The iceberg model

The issue of perspectives (as discussed in section 2.1) is an essential aspect of systems thinking. We must apply quantitative measurement to qualitative value when considering this idea. In other words, some elements of improvement-related innovation will directly result from quantitative measurements, such as the number of incidents or specific high-priority events. These are directly observable, measurable, and countable.

For other types of measurement, capturing perspectives or expectations requires something different. We recommend using Likert scales[3] or similar tools to quantify the qualitative. This approach allows us to collect and analyze things that are difficult or impossible to measure accurately. For example, we can get an absolute count of the number of incidents; we can't collect (i.e., by counting or some other enumeration) quantified data about the satisfaction with how well the organization responded to those incidents with the same level of precision.

The iceberg model tool (Cunliff, 2018; Figure 2.2) lets us better grasp system dynamics. As noted in section 2.1: "The perspective of the system depends on the view of the system, which in some cases might be limited to a few simple subsystems of the whole." In other words, if an individual's perspective of the system is limited to any subset of the whole, their view represents the tip of the iceberg – there's much more. The iceberg model looks at four levels:

- **Events** A perceived snapshot of immediate occurrences; potential symptoms of underlying issues
  What just happened?

- **Patterns** Trend or behavior over time
  What is the behavior over time?

- **Structures** Influences on the patterns; pattern/trend connections
  What influenced the patterns?

- **Mental models** Beliefs, attitudes, or assumptions
  What beliefs, attitudes, and assumptions exist about the system?
  What beliefs, attitudes, and assumptions keep the system in place (static)?

---

3   Wikipedia (2024d): e.g., on a scale of 1 to 6, do you agree or disagree with X?

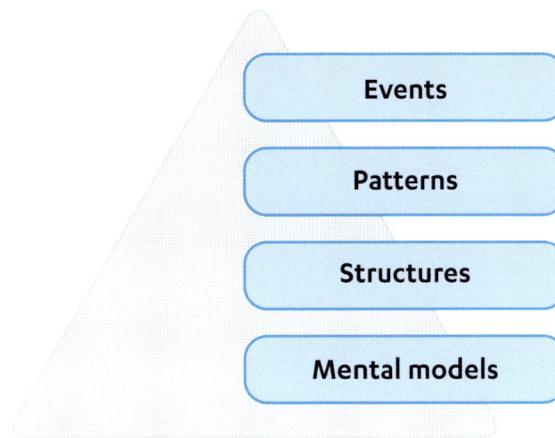

Figure 2.2 The iceberg model

Application of the iceberg model requires asking questions – questions that might not have been previously considered:

- What happened? What are the events that occurred?
- Either continue with questions about the behavior over time or plot them in a behavior-over-time graph (Kim, 2018) if the visualization would help
- How does the system structure influence or contribute to the pattern of events?
- What assumptions were made about the system? What are the beliefs and attitudes that form the basis of the assumptions?
- Is there anything missing? What did we miss?

This last pair of questions relates to an idea: How do we know? How can we be sure?

Questions originate from our mental models. To change a mental model, we must (a) recognize it and (b) ask different questions that explore different options. This concept is part of the guidance provided by using the iceberg model.

2.1.2 System structure and behavior

When you are building a box or organizing a company, the **system structure** addresses how you put everything together. You determine the placement of each part, how the parts are connected, and what functions they serve. If you arrange (or design) these components haphazardly, it is unlikely that you will achieve the desired results. In essence, the system structure serves as the blueprint for the organization; the design of the system impacts the behavior within the system.

When you attempt to execute an objective, the resulting interactions (**system behaviors**) within your system are constrained by its structure. If you have designed your organization well, the outcome will be as expected. But if the structure is faulty, the result will be very different from what you planned.

The relationship between system structure and system behavior is like a cause-and-effect story. The way you set up the parts affects what happens when the system is in "motion" (i.e., doing something – even if that's waiting for some event or trigger). However, there's an interesting twist. It's not always possible to predict how the system (your organization) will behave just by looking at its structure. Small structural changes might lead to huge and often unexpected changes in behavior without a temporal link to cause and effect. Consider the single line of code added to a system to "fix" a bug that, at some point in the future, causes the entire system to crash.[4]

Understanding this connection between system structure and behavior is essential to understanding how complex systems operate. Systems are composed of interacting parts. The number of parts is not an indicator of system complexity; the system is not the sum of its parts. Instead, it's the nature and number of interactions between and among the parts that make a system complex; system complexity is a product (in the sense of multiplication) of the interactions between those parts.

Complexity is not necessarily a bad thing, particularly if it is well designed and risk-informed. For example, consider the internet: as designed, it is highly complex and equally resilient. The sending of a single message requires it to be disassembled at one end, transmitted, and reassembled at the other end – with the possibility that different parts (aka packets) may take different paths to reach the destination.

How can we use this idea and apply it to an organization? The answer is to understand a set of flows within the organization. Specifically, consider the following three questions:

- How does work (intellectual or tangible) flow from an individual or team to others?
- How does communication (including decision-making) flow?
- How does innovation (including improvement) flow?

Understanding these flows within the organization can provide valuable insights into its structure, regardless of what is shown on the organization chart. It's crucial to consider internal processes and the involvement of external partners and suppliers. A single delayed shipment to a customer or from a supplier can trigger a chain reaction of consequences that impact the entire organization. As illustrated by the example of a single line of code (mentioned above), even minor, seemingly insignificant changes can have significant operational and financial effects, highlighting the relationship between system structure, behavior, and business risk.

Consider another example within an organization. A small change in strategy can lead to substantial business risk. For example, at one organization, cutting the customer support budget by 2% caused a 30% decline in customer satisfaction. Another internationally known household brand cut its television advertising budget by 3%, resulting in a 10% drop in sales.[5]

Little changes can make a big difference.

2.1.3   Coaxing system change

"Give me a lever long enough and a fulcrum on which to place it,
and I shall move the world."
Archimedes

You don't "fix" a CAS; however, it is possible to coax it into changing its behavior via a well-thought-out application of leverage. The use of "coax" is deliberate and applied to the whole organization, treated as a CAS. In her paper "Leverage points: Places to intervene in a system," Donella H. Meadows (1999) suggested, "Magical leverage points are not easily accessible, even if we know where they are and which direction to push them. There are no cheap tickets to mastery. You have to work at it …"

---

4   One of the authors, in the consultant role, has seen this occur too many times at different organizations.
5   One of the authors worked with each of these companies under a nondisclosure agreement, which is why they aren't named.

As noted above, small changes can lead to substantial negative consequences. What happens when the object is an intended, positive change? Changing a CAS to achieve the desired results isn't always clear-cut. Any system, whether it's an economic or business system, resists change because of the intricacies of the interconnected parts. This idea means you cannot just focus on behavior: you start by understanding the existing structure and behaviors.

If you attempt to force a change, it's likely to lead to unintended consequences. For example, how often does forcing "cutting costs" lead to a long-term contribution to the bottom line? More often than not, the long-term effect is the opposite of the intent. Coaxing a system allows it to adapt and mitigates the risk of adverse effects.

This leads to the question of how to coax a CAS to change – and the answer is the leverage points mentioned in Meadows' paper. It's beyond the scope of this book to cover these leverage points in detail: for that, we refer you to Meadows' paper. We list them here, grouped by degree from low- to high-order:[6]

- **Low-order**
  - Constants, parameters, numbers – be aware of the risk of what gets measured gets done
  - Stabilizing buffers (in systems speak, "stocks and flows")[7]
  - The structure of these stocks and flows
  - System latency – specifically, the length of a delay relative to the rate of system change

- **Medium-order**
  - Negative feedback loop strength relative to the system impact addressed by the feedback
  - Gain driven by positive feedback loops
  - Structure of information flows – i.e., who has access to specific information flows
  - System rules – including constraints, rewards, and punishments

- **High-order**
  - Power to add, change, evolve, or self-organize system structure
  - System goals (i.e., the goals of the system)
  - Mindset or paradigm that leads to system goals, structure, rules, delays, and parameters
  - Transcending paradigms – in other words, recognizing the belief that the current paradigm shouldn't (or can't) be changed.[8] This idea can be difficult to accept because paradigms shape individual mindsets, which determine how people behave in any given situation. It's challenging to accept that what we thought was "right" (i.e., the current paradigm) isn't working.

    Consider the line written by Sir Arthur Conan Doyle, uttered by his immortal character, Sherlock Holmes: "When you have eliminated the impossible, whatever remains, however improbable, must be the truth." Sometimes, you may be required to acknowledge that the current paradigm is not working, requiring a complete reevaluation.

Getting the necessary buy-in to apply leverage is an aspect of managing organizational change.[9] This is particularly true as the order of leverage points increases from low to high. It also may require organizational leadership to "coax" and curate a different culture.

---

6   We also covered Donella Meadows' original (and shorter) version of these leverage points in section 3.2 of our book *A Practitioner's Guide to Adapting the NIST Cybersecurity Framework* (Moskowitz and Nichols, 2022).

7   System stocks represent the accumulation of resources, materials, or information within a system at a specific instance. System flows describe the movement or transfer of these resources or information over time.

8   This idea can be detrimental to the organization. Consider the case of Kodak, the company responsible for the invention of digital photography in 1975. Its inability to recognize the need to change its paradigm from a film and coatings company to an imaging company ultimately led to bankruptcy in 2013. For more information regarding Kodak and the inability to change paradigms, see Bixenspan (2023).

9   See various works by John P. Kotter, including a book, *Leading Change* (Kotter, 2012) and his *Harvard Business Review* article on why transformation efforts fail (Kotter, 1995).

2.2   Expressing the organizational culture

The conventional view of culture includes the concepts of a set of beliefs and the resulting attitudes, assumptions, norms, and values, a set of actions and symbols, and more. In short, culture is how the organization expresses its worldview through people's behavior based on their core conscious and unconscious assumptions.

Consider the following from *MIT Sloan Management Review* (Hollister *et al.*, 2021):

> *"Companies cannot realize the true potential of digital [value creation and concurrent value protection], embrace new business models, or implement new ways of working without supporting changes in organizational behaviors and norms."*

A *Harvard Business Review* (*HBR*) article (Groysberg *et al.*, 2018) bluntly discusses strategy and culture. Strategy provides a formal basis for achieving organizational goals. Culture underpins and enables strategic success.

> *"Culture, however, is a more elusive lever because much of it is anchored in unspoken behaviors, mindsets, and social patterns. For better and worse, culture and leadership are inextricably linked."*
> Groysberg *et al.* (2018)

Connect these two ideas, and it's easy to understand why some "transformation" efforts succeed and others don't. If leaders don't recognize their role in cultural change, attempts at modifying organizational behavior will not likely succeed.

Several models[10] exist to describe various aspects of culture. The model we believe is most useful for organizations is based on the cultural web (Figure 2.3) developed by Johnson and Scholes in 1992.[11]

The "web" framework has seven distinct aspects. Central to this structure is the concept of paradigm, symbolizing the foundational mindset that governs the thought processes of most members of organizations. Paradigm encapsulates the collective assumptions that shape the organizational ethos, whether acknowledged or subconscious. The other six aspects support the paradigm. Impacting organizational culture requires understanding how these aspects affect the paradigm and vice versa. Leaders can morph the culture by understanding and modeling new behaviors in each area to impact the organizational paradigm.

---

10   The *HBR* article by Groysberg *et al.* (2018) provides a model; there are several others.

11   This model was introduced in *Exploring Strategy: Text and Cases* was originally published in 1992. The 13th edition is by Whittington *et al.* (2023).

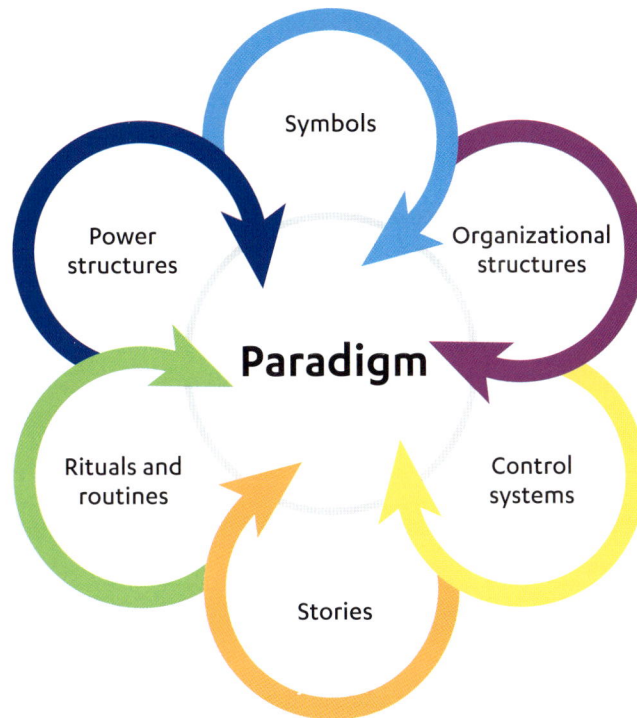

Figure 2.3 The cultural web of Johnson and Scholes

The other six areas of the cultural web support and underpin the paradigm, summarized as follows:

- **Symbols** The visual representations of the organization – its brand (and logos) and how it's presented, the perks and benefits provided to staff, titles, what you see when you walk into the organization, and more – that set the tone for the organization. What is the layout of the work area? Does it support productivity, collaboration, and transparency?

- **Power structures** The formal (represented by the organization chart) and the informal (represented by internal networks within and around the visual chain of command presented by the organization chart) reveal how work is accomplished. Expressed differently, power structures reflect how formal and informal sources of influence impact decisions, operations, and strategic direction. This idea represents the individuals (or groups) influencing outcomes; do they attempt to persuade or coerce?

- **Organizational structures** These are the formal roles, responsibilities, and reporting relationships. They are most likely related to the power structures described above. They describe how various organizational functions (hiring, budgeting, etc.) are carried out, potentially described in annual reports, and presented to customers and regulators. Is the reporting formally required or relaxed? Are all reports necessary for productivity and the production of value? How well do the organizational structures and power structures align?

- **Control systems** These describe how the organization monitors and measures performance and controls resources – either formally or informally. Control systems identify what's important to the organization. Do these systems address the quality of services (i.e., external focus) or internal oversight?

- **Rituals and routines** These represent what the staff members do and how they do it. This aspect of the cultural web includes activities, processes, and interactions. Are they taken for granted or regularly reconsidered with an eye toward improvement?

- **Stories** This is what the organization chooses to memorialize regarding past people and events. This is a crucial consideration impacting attempts to change organizational culture. It requires understanding that yesterday's hero could be today's villain to morph the culture. Stories also serve to highlight lessons learned or not learned. If you ask people about their organization, they tell these stories. Do they support ongoing innovation, or are they restricted to "This is how we do things here?"

2.2.1   Morphing organizational culture

Understanding the cultural web provides insight into what we must do to effect culture change. Use the web to understand the current and future states, which provides insight into what needs to change to achieve the desired outcomes[12] – with the understanding that it won't happen overnight.

Culture is more than just written policies or stated values: it's about the actual day-to-day behavior of individuals within the organization. It's observed in how people communicate, the decision-making processes, how conflicts are resolved, and how leaders and employees interact. It's also influenced by external factors, such as technological advancements and societal shifts, which can force modifications and adaptations to cultural elements.

You cannot directly change the cultural web paradigm (at the center of the diagram in Figure 2.3): you can only affect it by "nibbling at the edges" of each of the six areas.

Symbols are tangible representations of culture, like logos or office layouts. Employ leverage to change culture by redefining old or introducing new symbols that reflect the desired cultural paradigm. For instance, if innovation is a desired cultural focus, redesign office spaces to encourage creativity and display symbols of innovation.

Sample questions to consider:

- What are the semantics of expression (visual and audible)?
- How widely is this "language" used and known?
- What is the outside view of the organizational symbols?

Power structures within organizations define decision-making authority. To initiate cultural change, it might be necessary to change the power structures, for example, by decentralizing decision-making to give more autonomy to teams to foster a culture of responsiveness and innovation. This shift in power structures is instrumental in altering the organizational paradigm.

Sample questions to consider:

- Who has real power? How is this power used (abused)?
- Who makes (influences) decisions?
- How do these people act and demonstrate behavior within the organization?

Organizational structures, including hierarchies and reporting lines, can be a powerful lever for cultural change. For example, if the culture shift involves becoming more agile, adjust the organizational structure by flattening hierarchies and promoting cross-functional teams. These structural changes can facilitate the emergence of the desired cultural behaviors.

Sample questions to consider:

- How many formal management layers are there (how flat is the organization)?
- What are the formal lines of authority? What are the informal lines of authority?
- Is the actual decision-making aligned with the formal lines of authority?

---

12   The DVMS Institute, in cooperation with its publisher, TSO, developed a tool to enable organizations to evaluate their business risk culture. You can find more information at https://tools.dvmsinstitute.com/.

Control systems encompass processes and measurement mechanisms that influence behavior. Introduce new control mechanisms that reinforce the desired culture to drive culture change. For example, if a culture of sustainability is the goal, implement performance metrics and incentives tied to eco-friendly practices to encourage employees to adopt the desired behavior.

Sample questions to consider:

- Which processes maintain the strongest (most rigorous?) controls? Which have the weakest controls?
- How rigidly (loosely) is the organization controlled?
- What reporting supports "knowing" what happens in each department (operations, human resources, finance, etc.)?
- What rewards and penalties (if any) are meted out for good or poor work?

Rituals and routines are the recurring practices that shape organizational culture. To shift the culture, introduce new rituals that promote the desired values and behaviors. For instance, if collaboration is a desired cultural shift, leaders must establish regular team meetings or brainstorming sessions that encourage collaboration. Existing routines that do not align with the new culture must be reviewed and adjusted.

Sample questions to consider:

- What are the expectations when stakeholders (customers, suppliers, staff) enter the facility?
- When a challenge arises, what rules are applied? Are they documented and kept current? What happens if this is a new challenge; what rules are followed?
- What are the organizational core beliefs reflected in these routines? What behaviors do they encourage?

Stories are the organizational narrative history of successes and challenges. To influence culture change, apply leverage by fostering new stories that exemplify the desired cultural traits. Celebrating individuals or teams that provide living examples of the new culture is likely to inspire others to follow suit. Additionally, leaders should use storytelling to reinforce the importance of cultural change, encouraging employees to align with the new narrative.

Sample questions to consider:

- What stories about your organization do people tell (retell)? What reputation do these stories communicate to stakeholders? What do these stories say about organizational beliefs?
- What heroes (villains) appear in these stories?
- What stories do you tell to new hires? What stories will terminated employees tell about your organization?

There are several reasons why it's essential to strive to maintain a generative and supportive culture, including:

- **Cultural alignment** Creating a cohesive culture in an organization is crucial to achieving strategic objectives and retaining top talent. Cultural alignment involves aligning the behaviors and actions of employees with the organizational mission and goals while fostering a sense of unity and shared values within the workforce. This alignment starts at the top, with organizational leaders who model the behavior they expect to see from others
- **Employee engagement** Employees are more motivated, productive, and committed when they resonate with a positive company culture
- **Adaptation to change** The organizational culture affects people's ability to adapt to changes. A culture that embraces learning and innovation will likely thrive in a rapidly changing world
- **Customer and stakeholder relations** When organizational staff feel valued and respected, they will more likely treat customers and other stakeholders in a manner that fosters brand loyalty
- **Ethical behavior** Organizational culture dictates ethical standards in an organization.

There is a caveat regarding a supportive culture. Without ongoing active attention, it's very easy for cultural misalignment to occur, potentially without anyone realizing it until it's too late.

2.2.2   Leaders curate culture

Leaders play a pivotal role in shaping and curating organizational culture. They set the tone and ensure that all teams, groups, departments, and divisions operate harmoniously. They accomplish this by influencing and curating culture in the following ways:

- **Set the example** Leaders are role models, period, full stop. Their behavior and attitudes set the standard for what is acceptable in the organization. Employees follow the example leaders demonstrate, not what they say. Actions within the organization define its values. For example, when a leader demonstrates integrity and transparency, it's easier to promote these values as crucial organizational foundations
- **Communication** Leaders are responsible for communicating and modeling the desired culture and its importance. Through regular, clear communication and demonstrated action, they ensure employees understand the cultural expectations and why they matter
- **Hiring and development** In section 2.2.1, we discussed how a positive and supportive work culture can lead to a more engaged workforce and better talent retention. Leaders are responsible for making hiring decisions. That includes seeking candidates with the right skills and who fit the company culture. Note that "fit" does not address diversity, equity, and inclusion: that is a separate issue. In this context, it addresses how the candidate fits into the culture. For example, when there is a culture of collaboration, a candidate who espouses working alone or doesn't accept collaboration as an integral part of the job is not a "fit." Additionally, leaders should actively develop employees who embody the culture by providing training and mentorship opportunities
- **Adapting to change** Culture isn't static. In a rapidly evolving world, leaders must continually guide the culture to adapt to new challenges and opportunities, especially in the face of potentially disruptive technological advances (e.g., artificial intelligence), which requires establishing a culture of learning and adaptability – a learning organization
- **Handling crises** During difficult times or crises, a leader's response can, as needed, reinforce or reshape the culture. Ethical leaders uphold organizational cultural values in challenging situations.

Leaders demonstrate (i.e., model) the behaviors they wish to be pervasive in the organization – behaviors that are reflected by visible actions, communications, and decisions. They are the primary custodians of organizational culture. They profoundly influence how culture is expressed and adapted in practice.

In simple terms, organizational culture is revealed by how everyone (full-time and part-time, leaders, managers, and staff) feels about the establishment and consequently acts; it has nothing to do with how management describes the culture.

2.2.3   Culture and the Digital Value Management System

Applying leverage within these six aspects of the cultural web (see section 2.2) is an ongoing, holistic approach to change. Cultural transformation takes time and consistent effort. It necessitates leadership commitment, open communication, and the involvement of all employees. Importantly, it's about creating a deeply embedded new way of working and thinking in the organizational DNA. When strategically influenced, the interplay between these facets will gradually mold the organizational culture into the desired state, aligning it with evolving goals and visions.

In a dynamic world, culture is the unseen force that shapes organizational behavior and the interactions between the employees. Culture reflects the organizational personality, manifested in the way employees think, act, and relate to each other. It's a blend of traditions, values, habits, and practices reinforced and modified by the organizational history and the contemporary technological landscape. To fully grasp the importance of organizational culture, we need to define it, explore why understanding it is essential, and recognize leaders' pivotal role in its curation.

In the first paragraph of section 2.2, we say that culture is how an organization expresses its worldview. What does that mean explicitly? We use the term "worldview" to represent the mental model of shared beliefs, values, norms, and practices adopted by the staff and embodied in their work (see section 2.1.1). This idea includes their approach to problem-solving, the organizational stance on risk-taking, the level of collaboration, the commitment to innovation, and more.

The "level of collaboration" concept is pivotal when analyzing the dynamics within and between teams in an organization. It fundamentally questions the extent to which members of a team work together toward common goals rather than pursuing tasks independently. A high level of intra-team collaboration indicates a cohesive unit where knowledge, skills, and resources are shared freely to achieve the team's objectives. Within the team, this environment fosters innovation, increases efficiency, and enhances problem-solving capabilities as diverse perspectives converge to tackle challenges.

Conversely, if the work within a team is primarily solitary, this suggests a lack of interaction, or a highly specialized task allocation where collaboration is minimal or viewed as unnecessary. While this can lead to deep expertise in specific areas, it also hinders the team's ability to operate flexibly and respond to changing circumstances.

The concept also extends to inter-team collaboration, i.e., how different teams work together. Do they operate in silos, focusing only on their specific objectives without regard for the wider organizational goals? Or is there a culture of collaboration where teams share insights, resources, and expertise to support each other's success? The absence of silos and the presence of inter-team collaboration are indicative of a unified organization, where the barriers between departments or teams are minimal, fostering a more integrated and cohesive operation.

It's critical to understand that culture extends beyond written policies or stated values; it encompasses the everyday behavior of individuals within the organization. This is evident in how people communicate, make decisions, resolve conflicts, and interact with leaders and colleagues. Additionally, it is influenced by external factors such as responses to changes in the marketplace, shifts in society, and advancements in technology.

How does this fit into the Digital Value Management System? The DVMS is a generic system representation of any organization overlaid on top of everything the organization already does. We'll have more to say about the overlay in section 2.3. The important thing now is this idea of a system with linked structure and behavior. The idea of the DVMS as an overlay is supported by the 3D Knowledge Model (Figure 2.4).

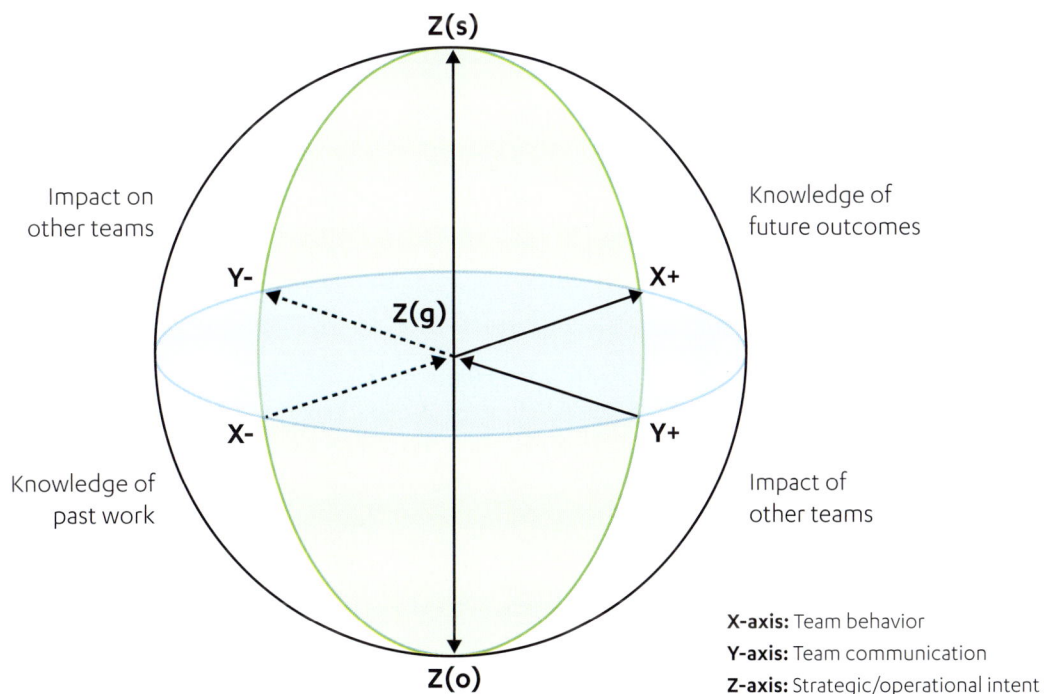

Figure 2.4 The 3D Knowledge Model

In the 3D Knowledge Model, the X-axis represents a single working group composed of individuals or teams. At each instant, the team knows what it has done (X- in the figure). It knows what it's doing (following the dashed line from X- to the center) and what it will do next (indicated by X+).

Again, simultaneously, the X-axis team needs to know how other teams impact its work (the Y+ line to the center of the figure). How does what the team is doing impact "me"? Similarly, it must also know how its work affects another team (that dashed line from the center to Y-).

Finally, the Z-axis represents the strategic (Z(s)) and operational (Z(o)) intent. That provides the constraints within which the various teams perform. The Z-axis also represents leadership and leaders' responsibility to curate the appropriate and expected behaviors. At the center of the diagram is Z(g), which represents the necessary overall managerial governance to both ensure and facilitate team collaboration between the X- and Y-axes.

2.2.4   A word about culture

"Strategy eats culture for breakfast."
Dr. Peter F. Drucker

We've talked about culture. Why spend so much time (and space in this book) on the subject? Consider the quotation from Peter Drucker above. The quotation does not suggest that strategy isn't important. Just the opposite is true: strategy is essential. However, even the "best" strategy will fail if the organizational culture doesn't support it. This idea is one of the reasons why culture is mentioned in various contexts throughout the book. Becoming a resilient organization requires strategy and tactics – the strategy must include addressing organizational culture rather than treating it as separate and distinct.

Both authors of this book served in the US military (one Army, the other Navy). We learned what it takes to build high-performing teams in that context and carried that knowledge into our work outside of the military.[13] Here's part of what we learned:

- **Examine every action** Anyone familiar with the military is familiar with the After-Action Report (AAR)[14] that examines what worked and didn't work during an operation.

  Takeaway A critical aspect of a learning organization is asking questions to learn and improve. What worked? What didn't work? How can we do better next time? What if something slightly different occurs; how would we handle it? Some agile approaches (or methods) call this idea a "retrospective"

- **Teams need autonomy to make decisions** Think about the life-and-death consequences if every decision and resulting action required chain-of-command approval.

  Takeaway Individuals (in a small organization) and teams must be empowered to make decisions – particularly where the scope of control matches the scope of effect. When the only person allowed to make decisions is some level of management "above" instead of the team, the implicit message is a lack of trust in the team

---

13   One author discovered that the ideas learned in the military had applicability to agile development. Both ideas are reflected in the list. An agile practitioner may recognize some of these.

14   AAR is a US Army report. Other services call it "Lessons Learned." Either name suggests providing a means to learn and improve information sharing.

- **High-performing teams depend on others** High-performing teams don't operate in a vacuum or silo. The success of any mission depends on multiple factors. In the military, there are various branches or "staff positions": G1 is responsible for personnel (outside of the military it's known as "human resources" [HR]), G2 for intelligence (understanding the marketplace), G3 for operations and training (training and execution), G4 for logistics (maintenance, transportation, supply chains), etc.

  Takeaway Every organizational "staff position" needs knowledge and awareness of the mission and responsibilities of the others. HR must seek people who fit the current need; resources (e.g., money, personnel, workspace) must be allocated to a project, etc.

- **Focus on outcomes, not outputs** Too many confuse outputs and outcomes. They are not the same. Outcomes represent the impact of a set of actions. Outputs, on the other hand, represent the immediate and short-term results of your efforts.

  Takeaway High-performing teams focus on the long-term impact of a set of activities. Consider the following: Launching a website is an output; determining the alignment of the customer expectations and reaction to the website represents an outcome.

2.3 The DVMS as an overlay

Frameworks are descriptive: they describe what to do, not how to do it. Methods provide concrete guidelines to accomplish something without necessarily providing a way to adopt or adapt them. In addition, frameworks and methods don't always easily scale – or at least don't provide an approach to scalability other than adapting or tailoring.

As we said in the introduction to this chapter, the difference between a framework or method and the DVMS is simple: the DVMS is not intended to be one-size-fits-all – as an overlay, it's adaptable by all, regardless of size. How is this possible?

2.3.1 What is an overlay, and why do we use it?

The DVMS is a generic scalable overlay that enables any organization to treat value creation and value protection as quality aspects, regardless of size. Every organization has or uses one or more systems, even if unrecognized. The DVMS is a generic system that can be overlaid over any organization, regardless of size. The best way to conceptualize this idea of an overlay is to imagine the DVMS being drawn on three sheets of very low-opacity tracing paper.

- The top sheet represents what the organization already has in place and includes frameworks, methods, standards, etc.
- The middle sheet represents the set of minimum viable capabilities (the MVC), briefly introduced at the beginning of this chapter
- The bottom sheet represents the means to operationalize the MVC encapsulated in the CPD Model, which we cover in section 2.3.2.

As noted at the start of this chapter, the set of MVC is an aspect of DVMS scalability. Everything the organization does falls into one or more of these capabilities. MVC scalability considers that the capabilities are not siloed: they are interconnected. For example, the Plan capability "bootstraps" the Govern and Assure capabilities.

2.3.2 The CPD Model operationalizes the DVMS Z-X Model

The Deloitte report on exploring strategic risk (Deloitte, 2013) contains the following (emphasis added):

---

*"Traditional approaches for managing risk tend to focus on monitoring leading financial indicators and the evolving regulatory environment. However, because they are generally grounded in audited financial statements, the resulting risk strategies and hedges are largely driven by **prior performance and past negative events** – and do not necessarily serve to detect future strategic risks or predict future performance. As such, **they are more focused on protecting value than creating it**."*

In broad terms, strategic risk looks at four types of risk:

- **Strategic** Risks created by or affecting organizational business strategy and strategic objectives
- **Operational** Major risks affecting the organizational ability to execute a strategic plan
- **Financial** Includes financial reporting, valuation, market, liquidity, and credit risks
- **Compliance** Addresses legal and regulatory compliance risks affecting the organizational ability to execute a strategic plan.

Organizations typically treat strategy and risk separately. Some split the two functions across two or more groups. Risk must play an integral role in the development of every strategy. This requires organizations to think differently. Consider a single entity: strategy-risk, instead of thinking about strategy *and* risk. We chose this construct because strategy and risk are inherently inseparable, like space and time. Strategy-risk supports the idea that digital business value *creation* requires *protection*. Simply put, any value not appropriately protected has no value to the stakeholder.

Take note of the last sentence in the quote from the Deloitte report: "more focused on protecting value than creating it." The essence of treating strategy and risk as a single entity, strategy-risk, combines the necessary looking backward (i.e., the lagging indicators highlighted in the Deloitte quote) with a forward-looking consideration that enables the organization to create and protect value.

The essence of the DVMS is linking strategy and risk to form strategy-risk combined with creating and protecting digital business value. These two concepts form the basis of the CPD Model (see Figure 2.5), which seeks to balance both aspects.

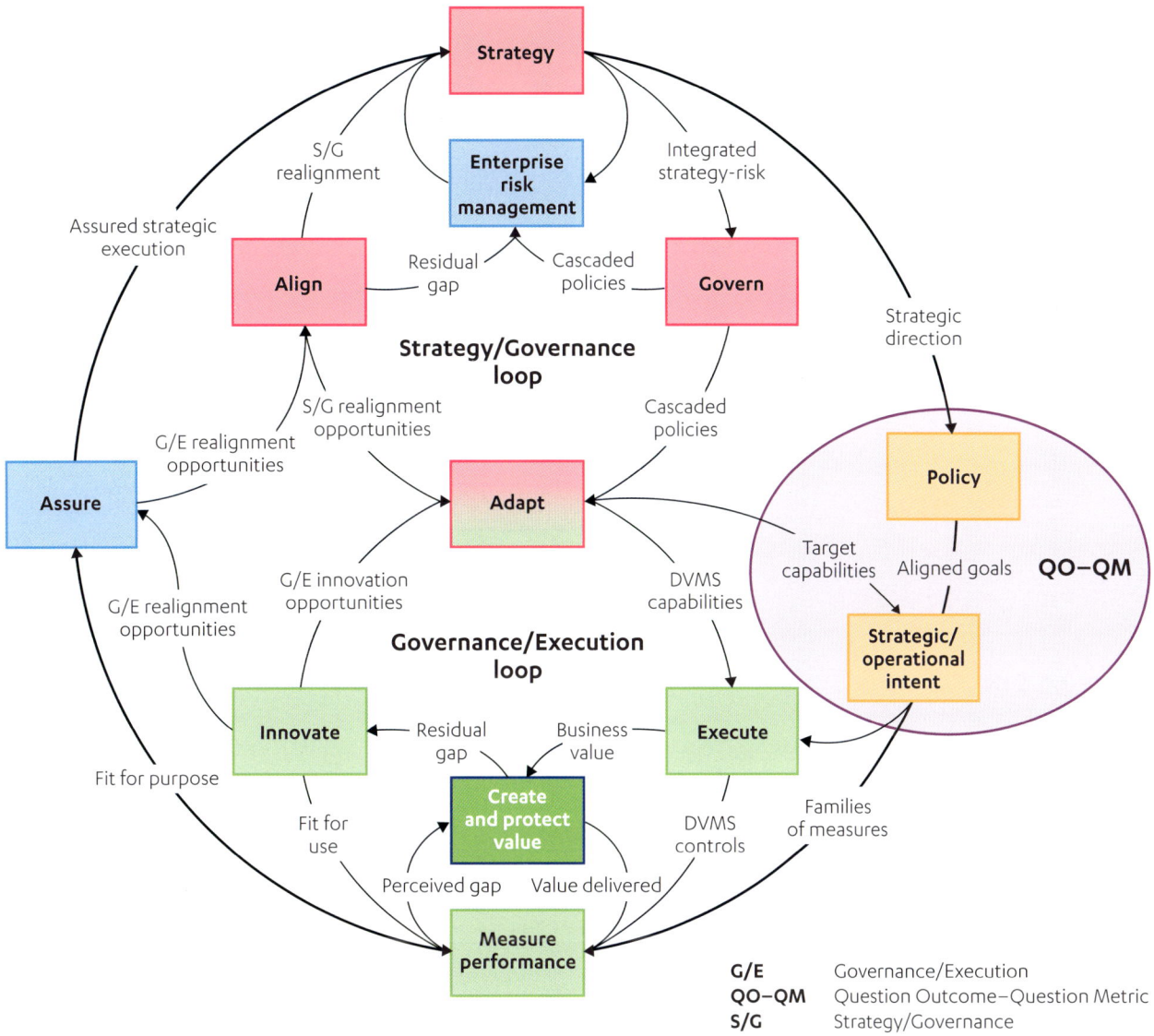

Figure 2.5 The DVMS CPD Model

The model looks complex; let's briefly decompose it.

2.3.2.1 Visualizing systems thinking

Before we dive into the model, we need some basics starting with the idea of a balancing loop (Figure 2.6).

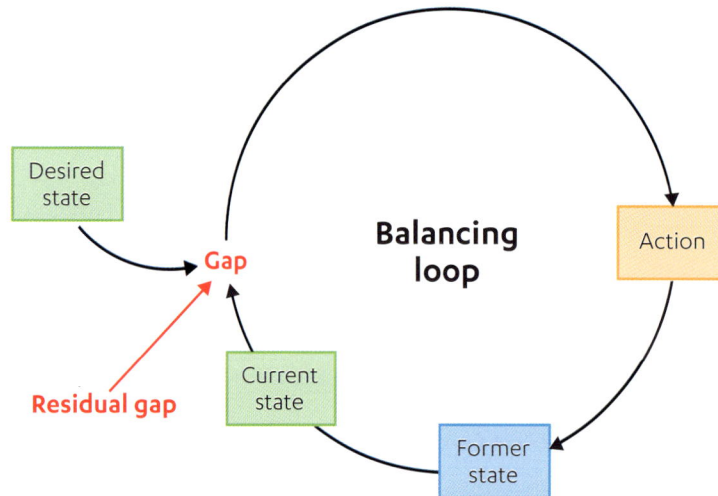

Figure 2.6 Balancing loop

The balancing loop assumes a gap between the current and desired states. Some action occurs to narrow or close the gap, creating a new "current state" that potentially requires reevaluation of the gap.

When you put two of these balancing loops together so that they "spin" in opposite directions, you get what is shown in Figure 2.7: an escalation archetype (Wikipedia, 2024c) (in systems thinking).

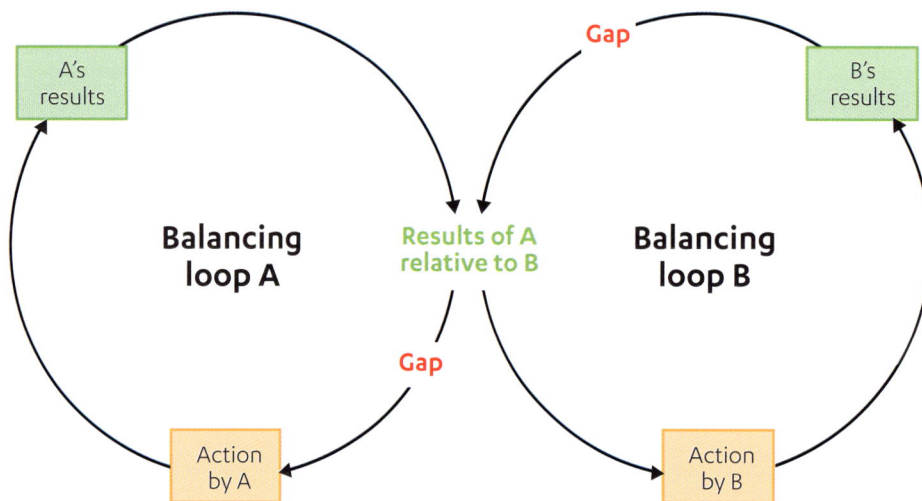

Figure 2.7 Escalation archetype

An escalation archetype is a structure of two balancing loops that interact to create a single reinforcing loop. It can reinforce positive or negative behaviors. To make this more obvious with a real-world example, consider the scenario depicted in Figure 2.8.

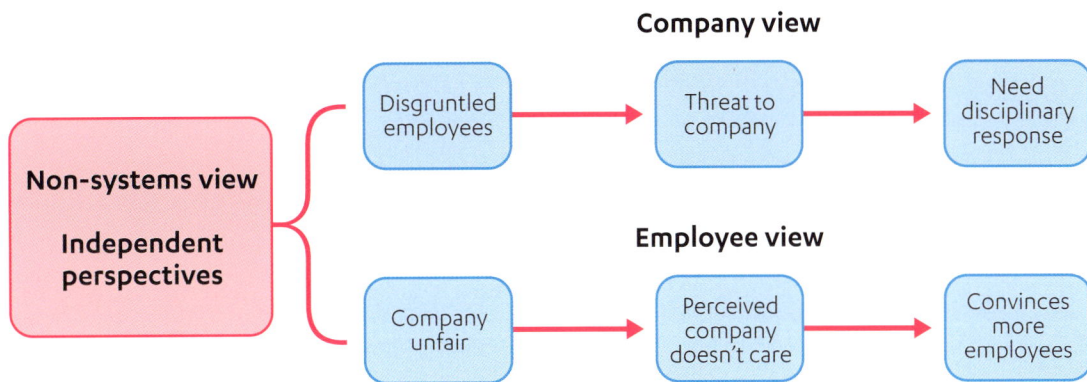

Figure 2.8 Linear and disconnected view of behavior and response

You may be familiar with this company where employees and management have divergent views regarding the factors contributing to a dysfunctional and toxic culture. When we change the representation from linear to two balancing loops and connect them in an escalation archetype, we get Figure 2.9.

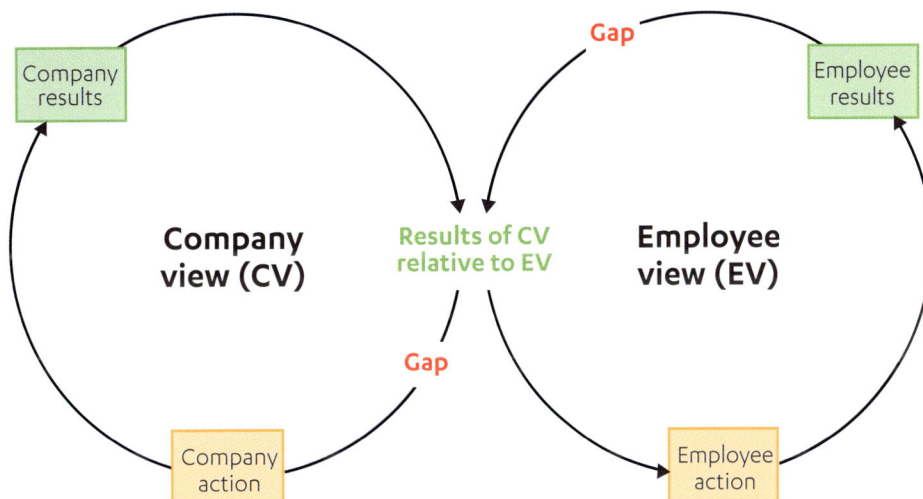

Figure 2.9 Toxic distrustful escalation archetype

Viewed this way, it's easy to understand how one group's actions reinforce the other's behaviors.

Now, go back and look at Figure 2.5. The CPD Model is a vertical escalation archetype with some added loops.

2.3.2.2 The CPD Model as an escalation archetype – decomposed

Now that we have a rudimentary understanding of the basis for the underlying model, we can look at the pieces. The Governance/Execution loop is at the bottom of the CPD Model (Figure 2.10). Note: in this and the subsequent figures, the discussion focuses on the colored shapes.

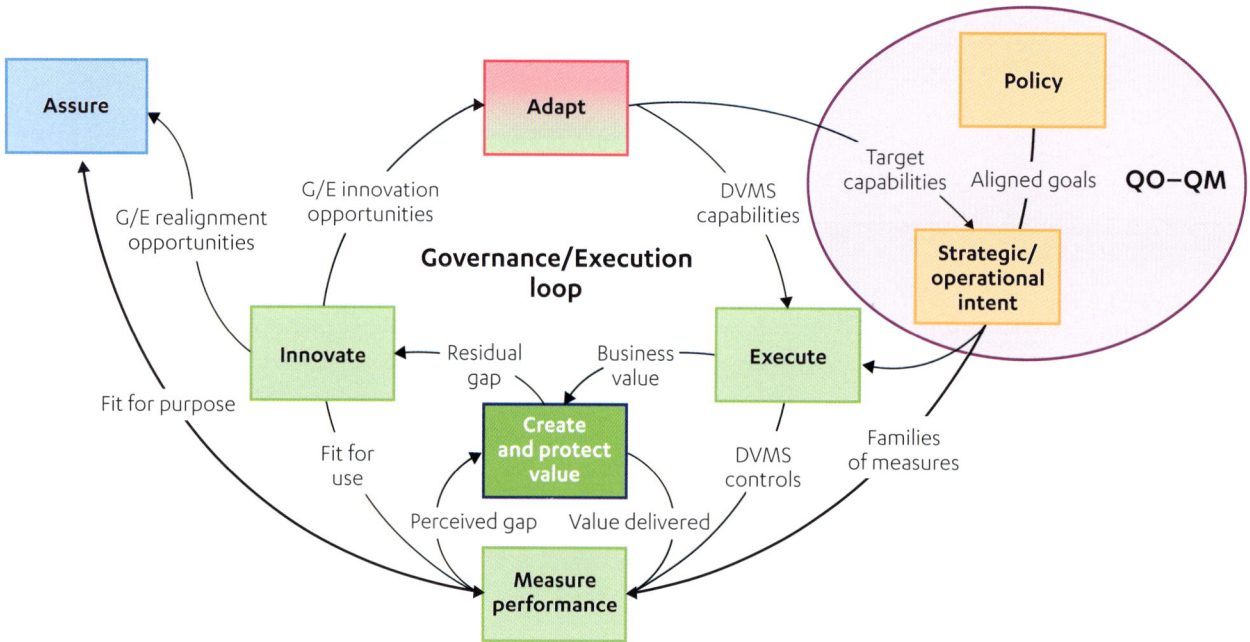

Figure 2.10 CPD Model: Governance/Execution loop

Regardless of size or organizational complexity, every organization enters the CPD Model at "Adapt," representing "start where you are" – the essence of an overlay. Start by determining both the current and desired outcomes. Use that information to identify the gaps between these outcomes.

This part of the model shown in Figure 2.10 encompasses various aspects of the DVMS minimum viable capabilities in the tactical delivery of digital business value. It also addresses the "small" incremental and adaptive innovations. It represents one aspect of potential organizational adjustments.

Figure 2.11 shows the impact of Assure and Innovate, and their potential impact on Govern. Note that "Adapt" is still an active part of this picture.

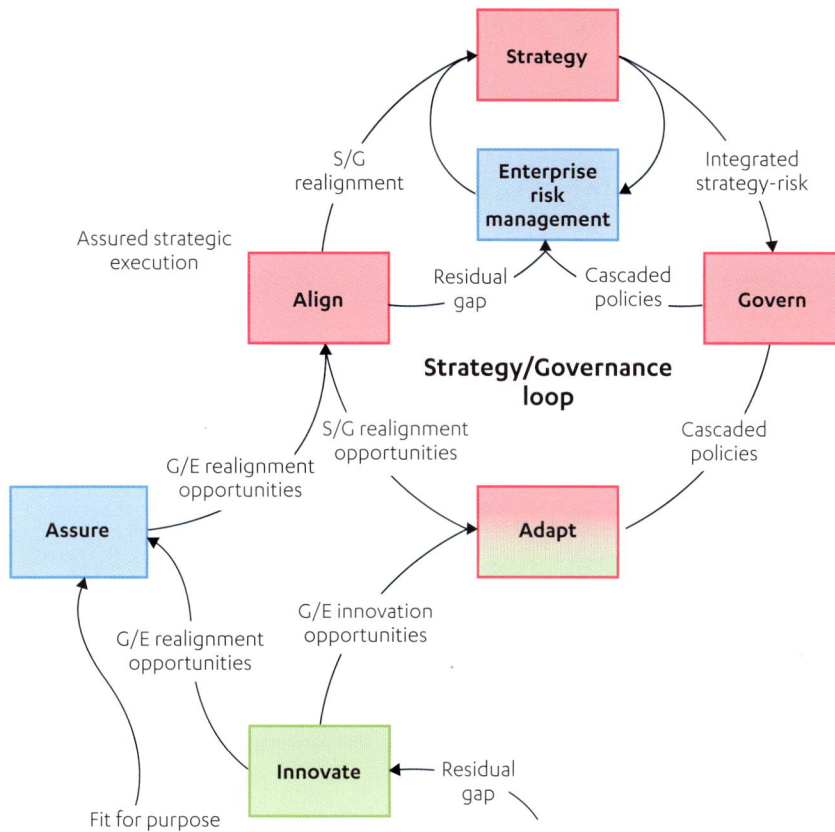

Figure 2.11 The Assure and Innovate capabilities in the CPD Model

Because policies stem from governance, this partial diagram represents an adaptive innovation.

To complete the relationship between the aspects of innovation and the CPD Model, consider Figure 2.12, which can also explain how adaptive and disruptive culture fits the model.

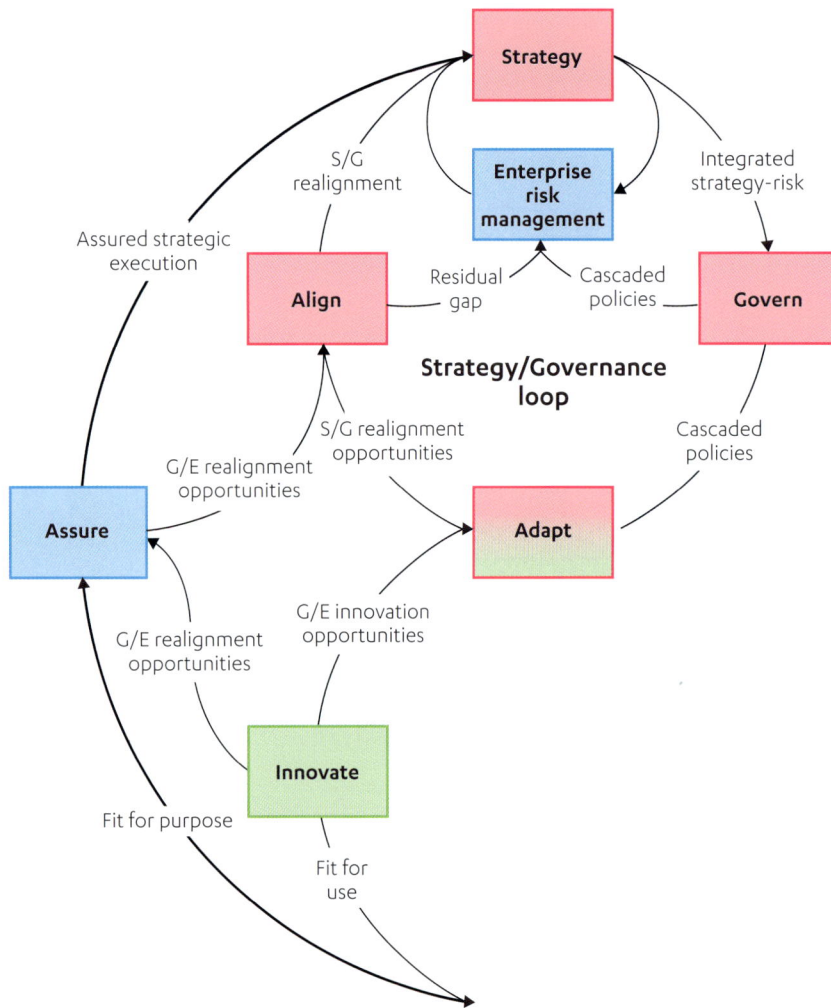

Figure 2.12 The CPD Model and adaptive and disruptive innovation

2.3.2.3 Question Outcome–Question Metric

There is an additional piece of the CPD Model that we haven't discussed: Question Outcome–Question Metric (QO–QM), which is our adaptation of GQM+Strategies® (Basili *et al.*, 2007)[15] to focus on the enterprise, not just software measurement. It is a question-based approach to ensure that outcomes and metrics align.

Proper application of QO–QM requires implementors (people who create value) and auditors (people who ensure value created is appropriately and concurrently protected) to work together to develop appropriate metrics that align with strategic and operational intent. The outer loop in Figure 2.5 starts with "strategy" and goes through QO–QM; this is where the metrics for both value creation and value protection are developed through the questioning process of both implementors and auditors. In this way QO–QM helps ensure that value creation and protection are treated concurrently.

The Strategy/Governance loop (top inner loop) turns strategy into policies adapted and executed via organizational capabilities, actions, and feedback that may cause a realignment of either policy or strategy.

---

15   GQM stands for "goal, question, metric." See Basili *et al.* (n.d.).

The Governance/Execution loop (bottom inner loop) turns policies into organizational capabilities that create, protect, and deliver digital business value. It does this by measuring and evaluating the organizational ability to execute strategic and operational intent that produces value for stakeholders, and to provide feedback from innovation opportunities acted upon in either the Governance/Execution or the Strategy/Governance loop.

2.3.3 Becoming resilient

How does an organization become an adaptive, resilient one? To answer that, we need to explore the concepts of adaptation and resilience.

"Adaptive" is the adjective form of "adapt," which means to adjust to new conditions. The adaptive organization adjusts its behavior to respond to changes in its environment. According to *The Merriam-Webster Dictionary*, resilience is "an ability to recover from or adjust easily to misfortune or change." The adaptive cyber-resilient organization must do both: recover from and adjust to new conditions.

The concepts associated with resilience provided the basis for our thinking that led to developing the CPD Model, which represents a complex system that enables digital business value creation, protection, and delivery. The CPD Model provides a systems approach to operationalizing the set of minimum viable capabilities (i.e., MVC or the Z-X Model – with the terms used interchangeably).

The Governance/Assurance loop is the outer loop of the CPD Model (Figure 2.5). The "Governance" side (shown by the Govern capability on the right) turns organizational strategy into policies executed to create, protect, and deliver digital business value to the organization's stakeholders. The "Assurance" side (shown by the Assure capability on the left) examines the performance of the organizational capabilities that execute the strategic policies to ensure those capabilities are fit for use and purpose. In addition, the "Assurance" side evaluates whether the value created is appropriately protected to meet stakeholder expectations.

2.3.4 Using the DVMS as an overlay

Using the DVMS as an overlay requires different thinking. First, as an overlay, the DVMS is framework- and method-agnostic – everything the organization already does maps to one or more of the MVC.

Second, every organization should apply the appropriate amount of rigor and coverage of the model. Think about this statement. Every organization, regardless of size, has an approach to strategy, governance, policy, execution, assurance, quality, record-keeping, reporting, etc. The degree of attention applied to each area depends on resources (including people, money, and time), industry compliance, and regulatory requirements.

Don't be overwhelmed by the appearance of the model. Regardless of size, every organization enters the CPD Model at the same place, in the center of the model at "Adapt" (Figure 2.5). You'll also notice that "Adapt" is colored (meaning "actively consider this block") in each of the decomposed aspects of the model (Figures 2.10 through 2.12).

Every organization should use as much (or as little) of the model as appropriate to fit its needs, with the understanding that growth and maturity require expanding coverage of the aspects of the model.

The CPD Model does not represent a step-by-step guide to change: it is a visual abstraction for the flow of communication, control, innovation, and work applicable to any organization. Some organizations will apply more rigor, and their associated flows through the model will be more detailed. Smaller organizations won't have the resources to assign discrete people to the various potential roles and responsibilities. They will, therefore, of necessity be less detailed in their application of the model.

Decide to adopt the DVMS and its overlay approach, and use it to understand how to adapt the organization to create and protect digital business value. Use as much, or as little, of the model as makes sense for the organization; but do so in a manner that enables expanded usage that comes with organizational growth and maturity. The CPD Model is designed to support both working in the system (i.e., consistent with producing organizational outcomes) and working on the system (i.e., consistent with improving organizational efficiencies and effectiveness in producing organizational outcomes).

2.4   Concepts of a phased approach

In section 2.1, we described the four fundamental principles, the second of which was "Change is a constant." We also included a "sub-principle" to understand that it was essential to work in phases and not try to do everything simultaneously. That's the essence of the DVMS FastTrack approach[16] – a phased approach to optimization and innovation.

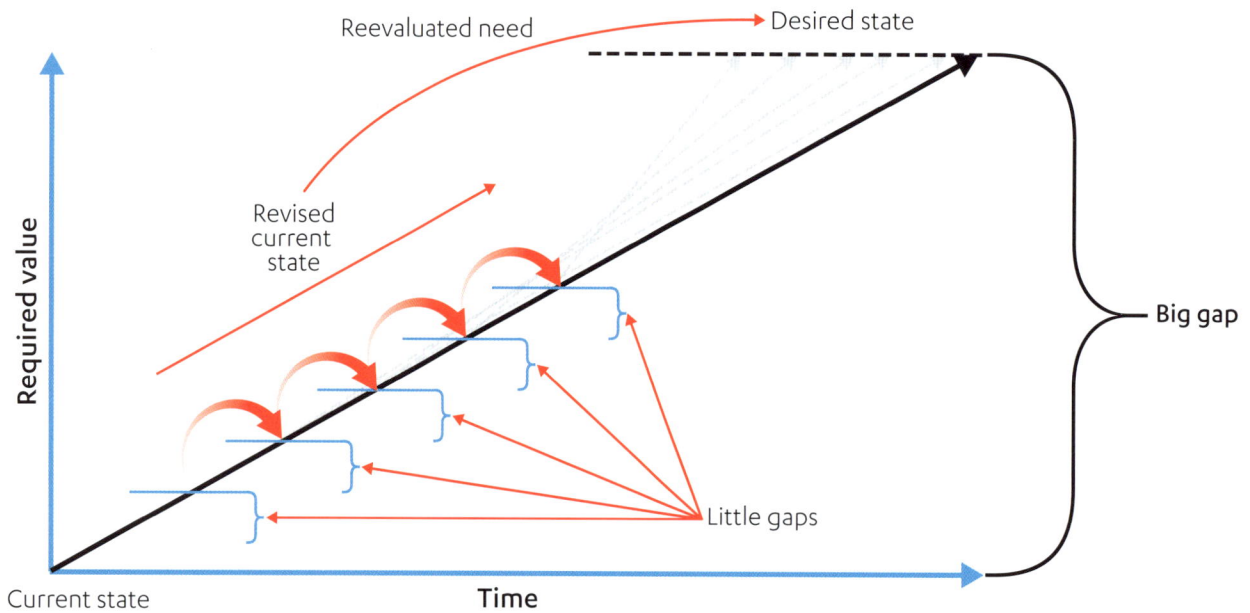

Figure 2.13 Little gaps versus big gap

Figure 2.13 presents the difference between working in little gaps (and phases) and big gaps. The dotted lines show an additive decrease in time to achieve the desired state following each little gap. Little gaps encourage experimentation. If the experiment works, you've made progress; if it doesn't, you've still made progress – you've learned what didn't work inexpensively compared with the big gap.

16   The DVMS FastTrack approach is a generic approach to agile. It's beyond the scope of this book to get into a detailed treatise on agile approaches and methodologies. If your organization is not applying an agile approach, several options exist, such as Scrum, Kanban, lean, DSDM/AgilePM, SAFe, Crystal, and RAD. DevOps, done correctly, represents a form of agile (though not usually at the enterprise level).

Working in phases helps organize the effort. Each phase comprises small iterative, incremental tasks and is executed over time. Complete a task and move on to the next; complete a set of tasks and move on to the next set.

The idea is to work with small (little) gaps that typically shorten the overall time to reach a goal, because, among other things, there is less rework and more stakeholder engagement during the process.

The DVMS FastTrack approach originates from agile approaches and the scientific method. The essence of agile is experimentation. Any agile approach and FastTrack are also consistent with Deming's PDSA[17] – Plan-Do-Study-Adjust – typically represented as shown in Figure 2.14. Note: to be consistent with our model, we changed "Act" to "Adjust."

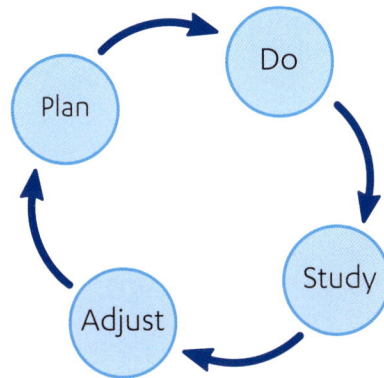

Figure 2.14 Plan-Do-Study-Adjust

- **Plan** represents the learning and planning required before doing something. From an agile perspective, think about this in the context of creating a hypothesis or an experiment for a "gap" (the difference or gap between the current and desired states)
- **Do** addresses conducting the experiment or acting on the hypothesis (in agile terms, build the minimum viable product [MVP] to address a portion of the gap)
- **Study** measures, evaluates, and validates the experimental outcomes. This includes identification (and potential reprioritization) of the next step
- **Adjust** represents the recommended actions based on the results from "Study." What did we learn, and how does that impact what we do next?

If you believe this looks reminiscent of Figure 2.6, you're correct. The visual representation of PDSA is a balancing loop.

2.4.1 Introducing the DVMS FastTrack approach

In the ever-evolving digital landscape, organizations must continually strive to adapt and scale their MVC to maintain a competitive edge and ensure the creation and protection of digital value. The course of action is challenging, requiring a structured and phased approach encompassing iterative, incremental, and interconnected stages. There are four phases in the DVMS FastTrack approach.

---

17   Some readers may recognize an older variant, PDCA: Plan-Do-Check-Act.

2.4.1.1   Phase 0: Get ready to get ready

The initial phase, aptly named "Get ready to get ready," lays the groundwork for the entire adaptation and scaling endeavor. It involves clearly understanding the existing organizational capabilities and identifying the gaps that must be addressed to achieve the desired MVC. This phase also entails adopting a systems-thinking approach to recognize and prioritize the critical areas for improvement. This work, and everything in each of the FastTrack phases, is performed within an organizational context that depends on size and resources.

2.4.1.2   Phase 1: Establishing organizational hygiene

Phase 1 focuses on establishing basic organizational hygiene, akin to securing a beachhead in military parlance. This phase aims to stabilize the major challenges identified in Phase 0 by implementing necessary measures to address immediate pain points and enhance operational efficiency. The goal is to create a solid foundation for further growth and innovation.

2.4.1.3   Phase 2: Optimizing and expanding

Building upon the stabilized foundation established in Phase 1, Phase 2 delves into optimizing the outcomes of the initial phases and expanding the defensible perimeter. This involves refining processes and enhancing the organizational adaptation of the MVC (including extending the MVC scope) to achieve greater effectiveness and reach.

2.4.1.4   Phase 3: Innovation for competitive advantage

Phase 3 marks a transition from adaptation and scaling to innovation. With a robust and optimized MVC, the organization can now focus on pushing the boundaries of its digital value creation and protection. This phase encourages experimentation, exploration of new technologies, and the development of innovative solutions to gain a competitive advantage in the digital marketplace.

The four phases of the DVMS FastTrack approach provide units of small experiments – a semantic license for "permission to make mistakes or have failures."[18] This might be new territory; by working in small increments and iteratively, the organization gains insight into what works and doesn't.

A note about the approach: iterative, incremental, and connected progression

It is crucial to recognize that the transition from one phase to the next does not signal the end of the previous phase. Instead, these phases represent a continuous, connected journey of adaptation, scaling, and innovation. Different parts of the organization may be at varying stages of development within these phases, creating a dynamic and ever-evolving landscape of digital value creation and protection.

As the organization navigates this phased approach, it should embrace the principles of iteration, incrementality, and connection. Iteration involves continual improvement and refinement of the MVC across all phases. Incrementality ensures that changes are implemented in manageable steps, allowing for adaptation and learning. Connection emphasizes the interconnectedness of the phases, ensuring that each phase supports and reinforces the others.

By adopting this phased approach and embracing the principles of iteration, incrementality, and connection, the organization can effectively adapt and scale its MVC, fostering innovation and securing a sustainable competitive advantage in the dynamic digital landscape.

---

18   This idea is like the "fail fast" concept central to design thinking and generic agile.

2.4.2 Curating an adaptive culture using the DVMS FastTrack approach

An organization must develop an adaptive culture to thrive as a learning organization. The phased approach to adapting and scaling the MVC provides a structured framework to promote an adaptive culture. This framework aligns with Peter Senge's *The Fifth Discipline* (Senge, 2006), emphasizing the importance of shared vision, mental models, personal mastery, team learning, and systems thinking.

Phase 0[19] is a crucial step in building an adaptive culture by establishing a baseline of the existing culture by examining the aspects and questions about the organizational cultural web (review the entire section 2.2). It provides an opportunity to ensure appropriate transparency regarding a shared vision and the potential to develop new mental models that promote open communication, collaboration, and a clear understanding of organizational goals. Phase 0 paves the way for continual learning and adaptation by identifying the gaps that must be addressed. In short, it sets a solid foundation for achieving desired outcomes.

In Phase 1, the organization aims to create a culture of personal mastery where individuals are committed to learning. This is crucial for achieving team learning in the next phase. The organization stabilizes major challenges and enhances operational efficiency to provide an environment where individuals can focus on personal growth and development. During this phase, individuals are encouraged to continually expand their capabilities and pursue personal goals while aligning them with organizational objectives. This phase provides the ability to address the initial cultural challenges discovered as part of Phase 0, noting that this is not a one-and-done: it requires ongoing effort to curate and maintain an adaptive and resilient organizational culture.

Phase 2 is a crucial stage that lays the foundation for cultivating a team learning and systems thinking culture. An organization does this, as noted in the Phase 1 description above, by optimizing outcomes and expanding its defensible cultural perimeter, thereby creating opportunities for cross-functional collaboration and knowledge sharing (see the description of the 3D Knowledge Model in section 2.2.3). This collaborative environment fosters team learning, enabling teams to identify and address complex challenges holistically.

The aim for Phase 3 is to foster an organizational culture that values innovation and adaptability. Individuals are encouraged to take calculated risks and challenge the norm by promoting experimentation, exploring emerging technologies, and developing novel solutions. This culture of innovation emphasizes the constant creation of new ideas, processes, and products to adjust to evolving market conditions.

2.4.2.1 Iterative assessment and leadership engagement

Adaptation, scaling, continual assessment, and leadership engagement are crucial for curating an adaptive culture throughout each phase. Iterative assessment involves regularly evaluating the current culture and identifying areas for improvement. This ongoing assessment ensures that the organizational culture aligns with the company's evolving goals and digital landscape demands.

Leadership engagement is equally critical. Leaders must model the expected behaviors of the adaptive culture, demonstrating open communication, collaboration, a willingness to learn, and a commitment to innovation – in other words, actively and consistently engaging in these activities. By embodying the values of the adaptive culture, leaders inspire and empower employees to follow suit. Suppose leaders do not consistently model the expected behaviors. That creates cognitive dissonance with the staff, resulting in the erroneous conclusion that "this stuff doesn't work," when the reality is that it wasn't given a chance because of the perceived disconnect resulting from "Do what I say, not what I do."

---

19   There is another aspect that starts with Phase 0 and extends to every phase that is beyond the scope of this book: the concept of psychological safety required to maintain the required level of transparency and open communication that is essential to an adaptive culture.

2.4.2.2 Cultivating trust: the cornerstone of an adaptive culture

Trust is the cornerstone of an adaptive culture. It provides the foundation for open communication, collaboration, and a willingness to experiment. By fostering a climate of trust, an organization creates an environment where individuals feel safe to share ideas, learn from mistakes, and embrace change. Trust is built by leaders who consistently "walk the walk" – aligning what is said with what is done.

2.4.2.3 Measuring and gauging cultural expression

Assessing and curating culture requires measuring and gauging its expression. An organization can achieve this through surveys, focus groups, and one-on-one interviews. By gathering staff feedback at all levels, it can identify areas of strength and weakness in its culture and develop targeted interventions to promote the desired expression of its worldview. Remember, culture isn't what someone says: it's about the reality regarding how the staff feels about the organization.

2.5 Chapter takeaways

This chapter introduces the ideas and concepts spelled out in subsequent chapters. Everything in this book stems from ideas grounded in systems thinking, including culture as an aspect of the organizational system.

We cover culture in the context of something relatively invisible, which does not mean it's not essential, just because it's typically expressed in conscious and unconscious behaviors. It's not a top-of-mind topic, but we contend that it should be.

This chapter introduces the idea of the DVMS as an overlay – not a one-size-fits-all framework or method, but something adaptable by any organization based on whatever it already has in place.

Finally, we introduce the DVMS FastTrack, based on generic agile, as a phased approach to making organizational changes.

CHAPTER 3
Mental models, leadership, leverage, and innovation

3 Mental models, leadership, leverage, and innovation

We've laid the foundation. We've explored the intricacies of systems thinking, understanding the link between organizational structure and behavior. We've delved into the power of mental models – those deeply held assumptions that shape our perceptions – and acknowledged leaders' crucial role in cultivating an adaptive culture that thrives on continual learning. Additionally, we've established the MVC – the essential building blocks (Govern, Assure, Plan, Design, Change, Execute, and Innovate) for navigating the digital landscape.

However, as the French writer Victor Hugo observed, "No dream is ever too high for those who have the courage to dream it." This chapter marks the end of the beginning. We've laid the groundwork; now it's time to build the scaffolding. Here, we'll delve deeper into the practical application of these concepts. We'll explore:

- **Mental models in action** How to identify and address limiting mental models that hinder progress toward digital resilience. The end of this chapter discusses the MVC (minimum viable capabilities) as a mental model
- **Leadership and the learning organization** Fostering a culture where continual learning is not just encouraged but ingrained in the very fabric of the organization
- **The power of leverage** How seemingly small interventions can trigger significant system change, and how this connects to the MVC framework
- **Continual innovation and self-organization** How to empower teams to self-organize and drive continual innovation within the established framework.

The dynamic digital landscape requires organizational leaders and staff to recognize and manage the challenges that must be overcome to deliver digital business value effectively. The DVMS provides a structured approach to achieving this goal by identifying and addressing performance gaps and fostering an organizational capability to understand complexity and manage the resulting digital business risk.

This chapter will equip you with the tools to translate theory into practice. We'll unlock the transformative power of the MVC and guide you on the path to building a truly resilient and adaptable organization that thrives in the ever-evolving digital world. Are you ready to embark on this exciting journey?

3.1 Mental models and organizational structure and behavior

To use the DVMS as an overlay, it is essential to understand and address new mental models crucial to supporting the development and curation of an adaptive culture that embraces complexity and effectively manages digital business risks. Mental models are the internal representations that shape individuals' responses within the organizational structure. These models form the basis for individual behavior and impact the organizational ability to navigate the dynamic digital landscape.

Our experiences, interactions, and interpretations shape our mental models. They act as filters that help us make sense of the world around us, influencing our decisions and actions. In an organizational setting, our mental models shape how we perceive the organizational structure, processes, and culture, ultimately affecting the organizational behavior as reactions to changing conditions, whether internal or external.

3.1.1   Understanding mental models

> *"Systems thinking is a discipline for seeing wholes. It is a framework for seeing interrelationships rather than things, for seeing patterns of change rather than static 'snapshots.' It is a set of general principles – distilled over the course of the twentieth century, spanning fields as diverse as the physical and social sciences, engineering, and management. It is also a set of specific tools and techniques, originating in the two threads: 'feedback' concepts of cybernetics and in 'servo-mechanisms' engineering theory dating back to the nineteenth century."*
> Peter Senge (2006)

A mental model explains someone's thought process about how something works in the real world. It represents the surrounding world, the relationships between its various parts, and a person's intuitive perception of their acts and consequences. Mental models shape behavior and set an approach to solving problems and performing tasks.

A mental model is a kind of internal symbol or representation of external reality, hypothesized to play a major role in cognition, reasoning, and decision-making. In 1943, Kenneth Craik suggested that the mind constructs "small-scale models" of reality to anticipate events (Wikipedia, 2024e). Mental models are cognitive frameworks that help us understand and interpret the world. Another way to think about mental models is that they provide a basis for "pattern recognition" to respond to a given situation – how our brains process information and identify recurring structures.

Here are some named examples, each followed by a short explanation and an example application:

- **The map is not the territory** Your mental model of reality is not reality itself. Example: Understanding that perception is subjective and may not capture the full complexity of a situation. Another way to state this is, "Your perceptions are your reality"[20]
- **Occam's razor** The simplest explanation is usually the correct one. Example: When troubleshooting a problem, start with the most straightforward and likely solution
- **Pareto principle (80/20 rule)** Focus on the 20% of tasks that yield 80% of results. Example: To ensure maximum efficiency, it is important to identify and prioritize the most critical aspects of a project – the 20% of effort that yields an 80% return (fix or reward)
- **Systems thinking** Understanding how the interactions between the parts influence the whole. Example: Recognize that changes in one department of a company can impact the entire organizational system.

Mental models provide a symbolic framework in which we make decisions – they provide a framework for thinking about and navigating different aspects of life.

The DVMS provides several key mental models – ways to think differently – that underpin effective digital value management. These mental models provide a shared understanding of the principles and practices necessary to create, protect, and deliver digital value.

---

20   One of the authors has a T-shirt that also address this. It reads, "You don't see the world as it is, you see the world as you are!"

Digital value:

- **Is a strategic asset** This mental model emphasizes the importance of digital value as a core organizational asset that drives organizational success. It also acknowledges that value is perceived (i.e., based on perception) and perceptions change over time. Digital value is not a product of technology: it is a by-product of the application of technology by people driven by strategic and operational intent of growth and innovation. This means that stakeholder value perception must be tracked to enable the organization to understand and adapt in order to sustain the value proposition

- **Requires holistic management** This mental model underscores the critical requirement for a comprehensive approach to managing digital value. Digital value is not confined to a single department or function. Instead, it requires a holistic approach incorporating governance, assurance, planning, design, change, execution, and innovation. It is based on the understanding that everything (including management and associated assurance) occurs within strategic tolerances that can and will change over time. This is an aspect of the systems-thinking mental model cited above – systems thinking is at the core of the DVMS

- **Demands continual learning and adaptation** The digital landscape demands continual learning and adaptation at the individual level, which contributes to, and is crucial for, team success. This mental model stresses the importance of embracing change, experimentation, and innovation to stay competitive and deliver sustainable digital value, with the understanding that the perception of value changes over time

- **Demands high transparency** This mental model requires organizational leadership to rethink how teams work and interact with complete knowledge and understanding of the organizational strategic and operational intent. Each team must know and understand its impact on other teams and the impact other teams have on it – with the acceptance that this is an ever-moving target.

More on mental models from Senge's *The Fifth Discipline*

Chapter 4 of Senge's *The Fifth Discipline* explores the laws of mental models. These laws can either inhibit or enable adaptation. By surfacing and challenging these assumptions, an organization can create a shared vision and foster a culture of continual learning, paving the way for individual and team mastery. We summarize these laws of mental models below:

1. **Today's problems come from yesterday's solutions** Don't just patch: understand the unintended consequences of past "fixes" to avoid creating new problems; anything else merely shifts the problem to another part of the system

2. **The harder you push, the harder the system pushes back** The use of force leads to resistance. Seek leverage points for subtle and impactful interventions

3. **Behavior grows better before it grows worse** Short-term fixes may mask underlying issues that will worsen later. This usually results from the application of "quick-fix" low-level leverage points

4. **The easy way out leads back in** Don't jump at (or assume) a potential solution (i.e., a quick fix). Instead, seek to understand underlying causes – solve problems; don't treat symptoms

5. **The cure can be worse than the disease** A potential consequence of the application of mental model 4 is a lack of understanding of the bigger picture, which often has unforeseen consequences. Look beyond symptoms

6. **Faster is slower** Rushing without reflection often leads to wasted effort and missed opportunities. Prioritize understanding and planning. See beyond the parts to the whole

7. **Cause and effect are not closely related in time and space** We've previously discussed this as a lower-order leverage point (section 2.1.3, system latency), and will return to it later in this chapter (section 3.3.1) regarding coaxing system adaptation. Consequences may appear long after introducing a cause, making analysis and solution design crucial

8. **Small changes can produce big results – but the areas of highest leverage are often least obvious** Seek hidden leverage points where small interventions can trigger widespread change. This is where the role of the four aspects of innovation (incremental, sustaining, adaptive, and disruptive) becomes an essential consideration

9. **You can have your cake and eat it too – but not at once** Trade-offs are inevitable. Design solutions that prioritize long-term sustainability over immediate wins while also pushing decision-making closer to the scope of effect

10. **Dividing an elephant in half does not produce two small elephants** Complex adaptive systems have emergent properties; separating them and considering them individually won't simplify their behavior – in fact, the resulting "solution" may make things worse

11. **There is no blame** Focus on understanding the system and finding solutions, not assigning fault for past problems – learning opportunities, not finger-pointing.

3.1.2 The relationship between system structure and behavior and mental models

Understanding system structure requires identifying the formal and informal[21] organizational components, relationships, and interactions. The hierarchical structure of organizations, with defined management and decision-making levels, reinforces mental models that emphasize control, top-down decision-making, and siloed operations. This approach hinders the organizational ability to adapt to change and effectively manage digital business risk.

Conversely, a more fluid and decentralized approach[22] that pushes decision-making authority closer to the scope of effect fosters collaboration, shared responsibility, and adaptability – also known as distributed decision-making. This approach creates an environment with different mental models where individuals feel empowered to take initiative, experiment with new ideas, and respond quickly to changing market conditions.

To understand how this applies to the DVMS, consider the 3D Knowledge Model, which we introduced in section 2.2.3 as Figure 2.4 and reproduce here with a slight variation.

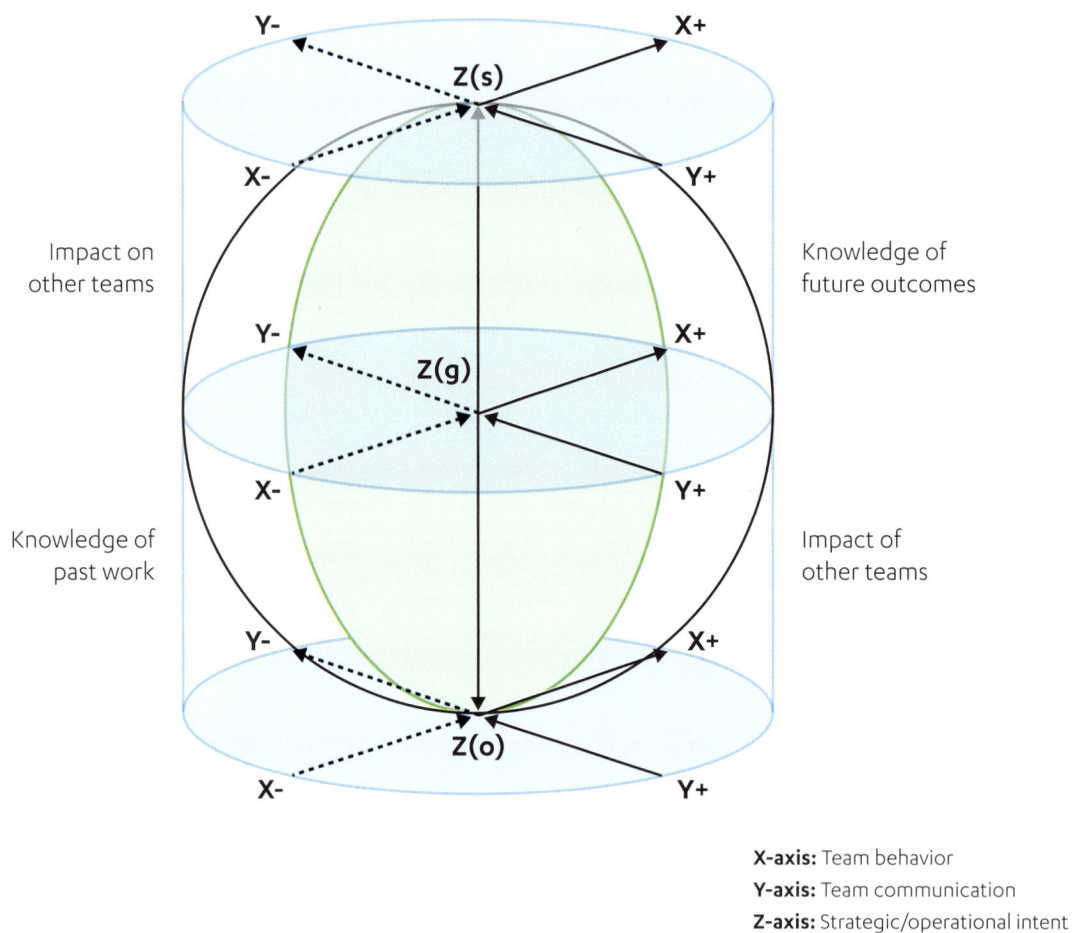

X-axis: Team behavior
Y-axis: Team communication
Z-axis: Strategic/operational intent

Figure 3.1 Stacked 3D Knowledge Model

---

21   See section 2.2 and the discussion of the cultural web for specifics regarding the formal and informal issues.
22   This description also includes the organizations that use a mix of top-down and bottom-up approaches – something that falls within the intent of "more fluid and decentralized."

Figure 3.1 annotates the remarks about the model in section 2.2.3 (Figure 2.4), adding two more layers indicating the involvement of more than one set of teams (including partners and suppliers). However, with the nearly full diagram,[23] we're going to extend the axes to suggest a broader view extending how the model applies to culture:

- The X-axis represents team knowledge of past, present, and future events. It is also representative of team behavior
- The Y-axis represents inter-team interaction that is part of the organizational structural controls regarding which teams can communicate with others and how that communication occurs. This is also an aspect of management
- The Z-axis represents the strategic and operational intent. This is the province of leadership to establish, communicate, and maintain.

By adding behavior, structure, and leadership, we've also defined how the 3D Knowledge Model supports an understanding of culture. Structure and behavior are aspects of the organizational system, and leadership shapes culture.

Understanding and addressing complexity requires recognizing the significance of mental models. Mental models can contribute to complexity by promoting individualistic thinking, obstructing cross-functional collaboration, or impeding progress toward change. Recognizing and addressing conflicting mental models enables an organization to break down barriers, encourage a culture of shared understanding, and embrace the intricacies of the digital landscape.

Organizational culture encompasses shared values, beliefs, and norms that guide how an organization functions, which are deeply intertwined with mental models. When mental models align with the desired organizational culture, this creates a strong foundation for effective communication, collaboration, and innovation. However, when mental models are not aligned with culture, this can lead to resistance to change, communication breakdowns, and an inability to adapt to new challenges.

Addressing mental models is not a once-and-done set of activities. Rather, it requires ongoing reflection, learning, and adaptation. An organization can consistently examine and address misaligned mental models to create a culture of continual learning, innovation, and adaptability. This, in turn, enables it to navigate the complexities of digital value management effectively and achieve sustainable success in the ever-changing digital landscape.

The 3D Knowledge Model supports this approach by adding the extra representations for each axis suggested above. The model also supports understanding interactions and resulting complexity that should lead to understanding the role of, and asking, different questions.

3.1.3 The role of questions

"The ability to ask the right question is more than half the battle of finding the answer."
Thomas J. Watson

Everyone knows how to ask a question. So why have a section about it in this book? The answer is relatively simple and may elicit a "Duh?" from some. You only get answers to the questions you ask.

There is a point to this. The better the question, the better the answer. Questions open doors to learning, growing, getting an idea, or improving ideas; they also enable us to develop a different perspective – an aspect of systems thinking. Questions help us interact and connect with others. Questions help us understand interrelationships and boundaries – two more aspects of systems thinking.

---

23 Note: The Y-axis interactions between layers are omitted to keep the diagram relatively simple.

There are many different types of questions, with the following short examples:

- **Evaluative questions** seek a conclusion or opinion ("What would happen if ...?")
- **Explanation questions** seek clarity and understanding ("Why is this the best way to accomplish ...?")
- **Factual questions** are simple and easy ("Is this correct?")
- **Reflexive questions** address self-reflection ("What can I do to improve ...?").

We ask questions for different purposes, such as:

- Opening doors
- Connecting and engaging with others
- Generating or improving ideas.

For our purposes, it is essential to ask open-ended questions, i.e., questions that cannot be answered by a simple "yes" or "no."

Using this approach, we started with a simple question based on the assumption that the picture of organizations was incomplete: "What's missing?" This question led to other "Wh" questions, such as "Why ...?," "What else ...?," and "Who should ...?" Our focus then turned to the last two purposes listed above: improving ideas and developing a different perspective.

It's critical to consider how to ask a question. Consider this simple example:

> *Can we do this?*

This question addresses capability. The typical answer is a simple choice of three possibilities (and variants): "yes," "no," or "maybe."

If we change the question slightly by adding a single word, we radically alter the intent:

> *How can we do this?*

This question addresses the development of a method. The assumption in this question is different: we assume we can do something and seek a way to accomplish it.

Avoid asking accusatory questions as part of the approach to asking different questions. For example, "Why did you do this?" accuses; "Can you help me understand why you did this?" does not – it collaborates.

You've probably heard the adage about repeating the same steps, expecting a different result, as a definition of insanity. You must approach the questions with a new perspective if you want different results. This idea is part of systems thinking: thinking differently.

- What do we do to create and protect digital business value?
- What do staff, partners, suppliers, and customers think about our culture? What can we do to assess our culture to validate the answer(s) to the previous question? What do we do to/with messengers? Do we encourage them or something else?
- What can we do to identify the components of our ability to deliver digital business value? What is the appropriate level of protection?
- How do we know? Are we sure? (Ask these last two questions in response to the answers above. They also establish the predicate for assurance.)

There are many more possible questions.

The last question, "Are we sure?" is less about the answer to the question and more about the delivery of the answer. More work is needed if there is hesitancy or the voicing isn't convincing. The purpose of this last pair of questions is less about rote or quick answers than it is about challenging assumptions. Acceptance of the answers expresses a risk-informed approach.

These last two questions also form the basis for the organization to revise and adjust actions and assumptions that underlie the current mental models. In more scientific terms, this idea is at the core of "double-loop learning." You can find a practical example in the retrospective performed by organizations demonstrating good-to-excellent agile practices when the team asks:

- What worked?
- What didn't work?
- What can we do to improve?

These questions provide a basis for double-loop learning by adding two additional questions: Are our assumptions about "this challenge" still valid? If not, what needs to change? Followed by the pair: How do we know? How can we be sure?

3.1.4   Understanding GQM to apply QO–QM

As its name suggests, there are three parts to the goal, question, metric (GQM) approach:

- **Goal** The conceptual level from a specific point of view
- **Question** The operational-level questions that need to be answered to achieve the goal
- **Metric** The quantitative level associated with each question.

The overall purpose of GQM is to ensure that you have the appropriate metrics to answer the questions that support the achievement of the goal. Using GQM applies a circular approach to refine all three parts (see Figure 3.2).

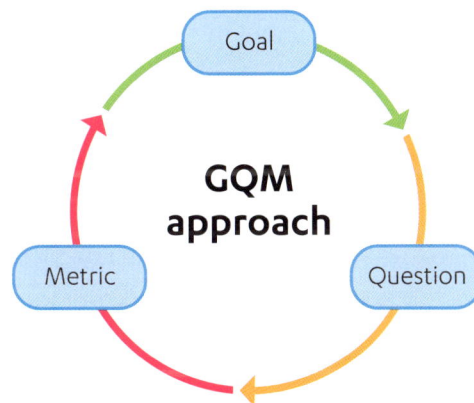

Figure 3.2 Goal, question, metric circular flow

Define **goals** for products, practices, resources, and other areas. Anything that requires useful metrics is a candidate for GQM. Goals represent targets for achievement and define a gap. The best way to create goals for GQM is in a team, not individually. Why is this so? We've discussed the importance of cross-domain teams without using this specific nomenclature, in the context of implementors and auditors working collaboratively. This concept also applies to working through GQM. Cross-domain knowledge makes it more likely that the GQM team will include (i.e., not overlook) relevant goal aspects. Cross-domain GQM teams also ensure that goals represent the gaps subject to measurement.

Questions address the operational level of GQM. Goals are not cast in concrete: creating questions may lead to goals being revised (Figure 3.2). Questions have a quantifiable basis – you will create metrics to answer the questions. A quantifiable basis supports quantitative and qualitative questions, provided that there is a basis to quantify the answer (e.g., using Likert scales). Questions also serve to support buy-in for the goal, if appropriate.

Metrics answer quantitative questions that will support your understanding of how you will know whether you've achieved an aspect of the goal. Approach the creation of metrics from the systems-thinking perspective. Avoid local optimizations, focusing on the part of the task instead of the product or outcomes.

Metrics come in two forms: quantitative/objective and qualitative/subjective. Objective metrics have a measurable value, e.g., hours spent on task X, or documentation exists to support a specific aspect of the goal (true/false). Subjective metrics require a point of view expressed in the goal. In the same way that questions may lead to refining the goal, analyzing the questions may also lead to refining.

Any metric may apply to multiple questions without having to be rewritten.

3.1.4.1 General GQM template

If you're familiar with agile *stories*, you have one possible way to start the process of writing goals. An agile story takes the following form:

As a _____, I want to _____ so that ____ (as determined or measured by or within tolerance of _____).

The first two parts of this statement represent the goal and the point of view. The third part addresses the issue or object. The last part addresses a start toward creating metrics.

3.1.4.2 How to use GQM

The overall GQM flow starts with assembling the right people for the team with appropriate cross-domain knowledge. The next step is to create and agree on the goals. With the goals at hand, write the qualitative and quantitative questions for the first goal. From the questions, derive the metrics. Review the whole set of metrics and revise it as needed. Then repeat for the next goal.

Record the metrics and establish an infrastructure to support the measurement program. It is essential to treat measurement as an integral part of project activities. As measurement data arrives, analyze it, focusing on the goals. Are things progressing within tolerances? If so, keep going; if not, take appropriate action.

Recall that goals should have a point of view. The point of view establishes the roles that interpret the result – this is essential for qualitative questions.

Use GQM metrics only to support the determination and achievement of the associated goals; using the resulting metrics outside of a GQM context is not the intent of the approach, and may lead to unintended consequences.

Figure 3.3 illustrates the relationship between the three parts of GQM. Notice the bottom two metrics each relate to more than one question.

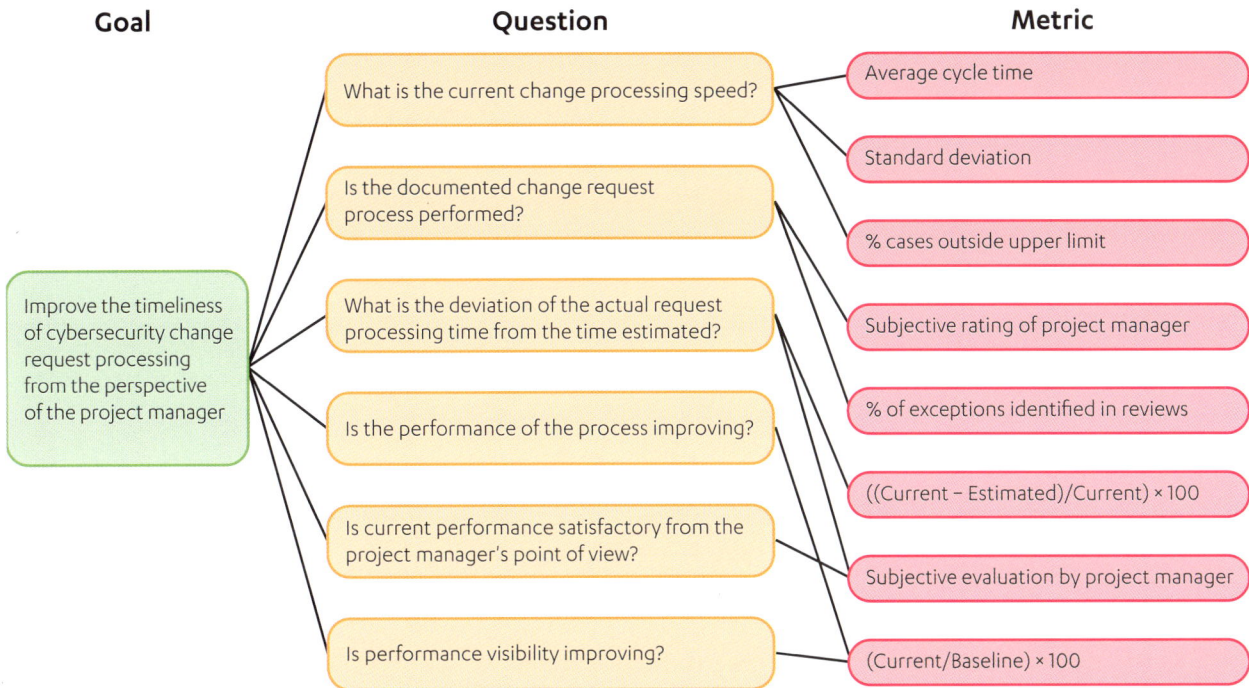

Figure 3.3 GQM example mapping of goals to questions to metrics

When does it make sense to use GQM? This question is answered by understanding the use cases for GQM. While many people think use cases are for software development, they originated in the telecommunications industry. They apply to anything with interactions between entities (called *actors* or *systems*).

3.1.5 Using Question Outcome–Question Metric

Change is a constant. While this statement might seem like an oxymoron, it highlights a critical fact: the organizational ability to change must be a core, mission-critical capability. QO–QM provides means to link strategy-risk intent with its operational execution. It supports creating new mental models that form the basis for new event responses.

Successful implementation depends on ensuring the alignment between strategy-risk and operational intent. QO–QM links strategy with appropriate operational measures and metrics. Input to QO–QM in the CPD Model includes the policies generated in the Strategy/Governance loop. The output of QO–QM provides input to the alignment of strategic and operational intent that guides the measurement and metrics critical to the Governance/ Execution loop.

From this perspective, QO–QM enables the auditor and implementor to develop appropriate metrics representative of their points of view (POV). Integrating the 3D Knowledge Model allows combining the perspectives of working *on* the system and working *in* the system.

This approach provides clarity and focuses on the delivery and protection of digital business value. It seeks feedback to understand value gaps, assuming that there are two change-related issues: external change causing an organizational reaction, and the critical internal core mission capability to change.

3.1.5.1 Strategy-risk

The CPD Model treats risk as an intrinsic aspect of strategy – encapsulated in the concept of strategy-risk as a single entity. An organization *must* adopt an enterprise risk management (ERM) framework to make its business strategy risk-informed. The basis for the CPD Model is simple: every aspect of strategy requires an understanding of risk. The model presents the idea as a single concept, "strategy-risk." Like "space-time," the two elements of strategy-risk exist together and cannot be separated.

QO–QM is fundamental for developing the link between strategic and operational intent. Later, in the Governance/Execution loop, we'll see how the measures and metrics identified here are used to instrument the DVMS to capture the desired metrics. The Governance/Execution and Strategy/Governance loops create the dynamic capability of the CPD Model to continually seek to minimize gaps in strategy-risk, policies, DVMS, and the creation, protection, and delivery of digital business value.

QO–QM is an approach that ensures the alignment of strategic outcomes. It develops the measures and metrics to assess the delivered digital business value against the expressed strategic and operational intent. Assess performance gaps to determine opportunities to improve (incremental) or innovate (disruptive) the delivery of digital business value. Remember that the 3D Knowledge Model is essential to the CPD Model and applying QO–QM.

3.1.5.2 Question Outcome–Question Metric explained

During the height of the Covid-19 pandemic, one of the authors was asked what was the best and easiest skill to learn if you want to do something in cybersecurity. The answer included the following:

> *In response to the question "What's the best and easiest skill to learn in (substitute any skill here)?" the answer is the same. "You've already started. You asked a question. Perhaps one of the most important skills everyone needs to learn is to ask better questions."*

As noted in section 3.1.3, you only get answers to the questions you ask. If you want better answers, you must ask better questions. In that section, we suggested a partial list of purposes for asking questions:

- Opening doors
- Connecting and engaging with others
- Generating or improving ideas.

For QO–QM, we add another:

- Seeking to verify and validate an outcome that might include potentially understanding or developing a different perspective to get out of a rut.

This approach and additional thought led to the development of QO–QM. Operating within the context of the CPD Model, seeing the organization as a whole requires avoiding questions that lead to thinking such as "Can we do X?" We need to ask different questions that enable us to focus on the whole.

Questions that ask about an outcome in the context of the 3D Knowledge Model:

- How does the outcome for team A impact (or how is it impacted by) team B?
- How does the Z-axis impact the outcome?

Questions that address strategy-risk – not just what is the risk, but what are the thresholds:

- When (not if) something happens, what is the organizational risk?
  - If the event impact exceeds the organizational tolerances, how do we respond? What can we learn?
  - If the event impact is within tolerances, what can we learn? Do we need to adjust the tolerances? And so on

- How does this event impact the development teams?

QO–QM is GQM with an added set of questions designed to link strategy-risk[24] with business outcomes. Start by asking questions about the strategy-risk objectives to clarify the outcome intent – the "O" in "QO–QM" represents the goal in GQM. The difference is in the initial questions that specifically address the goal in the broader strategic context as represented by the 3D Knowledge Model. Following the outcome refinement, QO–QM proceeds in the same way as GQM. While it is still possible that the quantifiable questions might lead to a revision of the outcome, the intent is to address the strategic fit first.

3.1.5.3 Question Outcome–Question Metric implemented

As noted above, QO–QM is a team activity that requires the participation of implementors and auditors. Before explicitly starting down the first stage of questions in QO–QM, assemble the right team that covers the various stakeholders potentially affected by the selected goal. The team members represent the specific technical aspects of the goal and the 3D Knowledge Model. The team should also include people representing the implementors' and auditors' points of view.

3.1.5.4 Tell a story to generate questions

It is possible to borrow from agile stories to form the questions associated with metrics. For example:

> As a ___(POV)___, I want to ___(accomplish something)___ so that ___(outcome achieved)___ as determined by ___(metric within tolerance)___.

This type of story leads to point-of-view questions regarding outcomes and the metrics. The associated metrics could be qualitative or quantitative. For example, from the users' perspective, is the performance improving?

If the point of view is not pertinent for this QO–QM (or GQM) outcome, change the story:

> When __(N)__ happens, we need to ___(respond or accomplish something)___ so that ___(outcome achieved)___ as determined by ___(metric within tolerance)___.

In this case, the issue is not about a point of view: it addresses an event. When X happens, what is the response, what do we expect, and how will we know?

Implementors ask questions that result in metrics with the context that addresses "what" to accomplish and "how" to do so; auditors ask questions that result in metrics that address "How will we know?" and "How can we be sure?"

The organization can change the structure or behaviors to bring the system output within acceptable tolerances.

Fundamental to systems thinking is the idea that there is variable latency between cause (behaviors) and the observation or detection of the related effect. Understanding latency enables better decision-making in effecting change in a system.

---

24 The practical application of QO–QM depends on the organization crafting unambiguous strategy-risk policies.

3.2 Leadership and a learning organization

An organization must prioritize managing digital business risk as a guiding principle with the understanding that it is not just a list of protocols: it involves building a culture that supports organizational learning and agility to adapt to change and ask different questions. This section explores how managing digital business risk, leadership, and organizational culture are interconnected to ensure success.

Building and sustaining a learning organization requires leaders who demonstrate appropriate levels of collaboration and cooperation. Leaders are the "walking examples" who embody the behaviors and values they expect from others – 24×7×365. This means embracing transparency, actively seeking feedback, and readily challenging assumptions (including their own). Leaders who "walk the walk" build trust, foster psychological safety, and encourage others to do the same. This behavioral consistency is also a critical aspect of trust that is a cornerstone of the learning organization.

> **Psychological safety**
>
> We use the term "psychological safety" to refer to the individual and collective feeling of a team (or workgroup) that supports taking interpersonal risks. In other words, team members know they won't be penalized for asking difficult questions, raising concerns, challenging the status quo, admitting mistakes, and so on. This "feeling" means that everyone is comfortable sharing ideas, even if they differ from those of the majority. People are free to voice opinions without enduring personal attacks (blame), worrying about criticism, or being subject to penalties.

In a complex and ever-changing environment, continual innovation is not just a luxury: it's a necessity for survival. To encourage innovation, leaders must foster a culture of experimentation, which empowers teams to explore new ideas, challenge existing norms, and develop innovative solutions to emerging challenges. This requires providing the necessary resources, creating safe spaces for failure, and celebrating experimentation regardless of the outcome. Only then can the organization develop the adaptive intelligence required to thrive and face constant change.

These ideas are just the beginning of the conversation. Let's explore the practical implications of this paradigm shift and delve deeper into how leaders can become true curators of adaptive cultures that deliver enduring digital business value.

3.2.1 Culture – whether you like it or not

The connection between digital business risk management (DBRM), leadership as cultural stewardship, and continual innovation forms a virtuous cycle. Leaders prioritizing DBRM create a risk-aware culture where learning and adaptation are valued. By "walking the walk" and championing continual innovation, leaders ensure the organization possesses the adaptive intelligence to navigate complexity, deliver optimal digital business value, and thrive in the digital age.

This shift in leadership paradigm – from command and control to curation and stewardship – isn't just about embracing new tools or methodologies. It's about fundamentally changing the way we think about organizational culture and the critical role leaders play in shaping it. By aligning with the imperative of DBRM, leading by example, and fostering a culture of continual learning, leaders can morph their organizations into engines of sustainable success in the face of any challenge.

An organizational culture is shaped by the underlying beliefs of the staff and the assumptions that are reflected in the organizational paradigm. This culture comprises the unspoken language, daily rituals, and unspoken rewards that influence how people think, act, and respond to challenges. As the curators of this culture, leaders must take responsibility for understanding how their decisions and actions shape this invisible ecosystem. By prioritizing DBRM (which includes data-based decision-making), championing open communication, embracing experimentation, and celebrating failures as learning opportunities, leaders can instill these values into the organizational cultural fabric.

Consider the three cultures model suggested by Professor Robert Westrum in his paper "A typology of organisational cultures" (Westrum, 2004):

- **Pathological** (power-oriented) cultures are typified by low cooperation and blame, where information is withheld to create or maintain personal power or gain. Messengers figuratively shot
- **Bureaucratic** (rule-oriented) cultures focus more on rules and chain of command, with compartmentalized responsibilities and a typical focus on fiefdoms rather than the overall organizational mission. Messengers ignored
- **Generative** (performance-oriented) cultures exhibit appropriate information flows and transparency with high team cooperation and trust. Messengers trained and encouraged.

Westrum doesn't provide remedies, just the classification and clues to identify them. We introduced a way to address cultural change in section 2.2. Identify the type of culture in your organization and use the suggested approach to help morph it, recognizing that culture isn't how management describes the organization but how staff feel about it.

There is one additional point to make based on today's reality. Digital evolution[25] is no longer an option: safeguarding digital business value through effective DBRM is essential. This risk-conscious approach goes beyond traditional frameworks and involves proactively identifying vulnerabilities in capabilities, resulting practices, systems, and cultural blind spots that could hinder the delivery of digital value. Leaders committed to DBRM empower their teams to experiment, learn from setbacks, and adapt without fear of reprisal, which are aspects of a generative culture.

In Chapter 2, we referenced a *Harvard Business Review* article collection titled "The leader's guide to corporate culture" (Groysberg *et al.*, 2018), which provides a proactive approach to classifying and shifting corporate culture. The article postulates applying eight dimensions to understand organizational culture:

- **Caring** Warm, sincere, and relational
- **Purpose** Purpose-driven, idealistic, and tolerant
- **Learning** Open, inventive, and exploring
- **Enjoyment** Playful, instinctive, and fun-loving
- **Results** Achievement-driven and goal-focused
- **Authority** Bold, decisive, and dominant
- **Safety** Realistic, careful, and prepared
- **Order** Rules-abiding, respectful, and cooperative.

The ideas suggested by these authors' diverse approaches to culture are not contradictory. Rather, they indicate different ways of examining and understanding culture. It is beyond the scope of this publication to delve into any of these in depth.

---

25   We prefer the term "digital evolution" to "digital transformation" because "transformation" suggests something potentially finite while "evolution" connotes something ongoing.

3.2.2　It's not just about cybersecurity

OK, the title of this section says it's not about cybersecurity. That's true. What it's not about is the *current concept* of cybersecurity. This isn't your father's cybersecurity. It is about this new strategy for managing business risk by focusing on creating and protecting digital business value as an aspect of quality – quality, not technology. With this approach, the organization gets cybersecurity as a by-product. How is that possible? Consider an example from an unrelated field.

A composer creates the score for a symphony. Until the conductor leads the orchestra in an interpretation of the score, it's merely notes on a page. We liken this musical score to an organizational strategy that provides a path to creating, protecting, and delivering digital business value. Just as the composer uses musical dissonance and counterpoint to add depth and tension to the melody, DBRM provides a reminder of potential pitfalls. Combining the score (the strategy) with counterpoint and dissonance (digital business risk) yields the idea of strategy-risk as a single entity – not strategy *and* risk, potentially in two different areas of the organization, but a single entity, because managing digital business risk, not just technical risk, is paramount.

"Strategy-risk" is the term we use to describe the balance between making ambitious strategic moves and the uncertainty about the outcomes. It acknowledges that such moves always carry inherent risks; effectively navigating them is key to success. DBRM recognizes the importance of managing risks beyond technical silos and transforming it into a strategic cornerstone that permeates every facet of the organization, which is how we get to quality.

From this perspective, the central idea behind organizational resiliency is a mindset change from creating *then* protecting to creating *and* protecting digital business value. This concurrent activity raises questions about how the value created is concurrently protected at an appropriate level – with the understanding that the "appropriate level" must be reevaluated in the context of changing strategy-risk.

It's not just about having firewalls and anti-virus software: it's about identifying and understanding the vulnerabilities inherent in business processes, data, and organizational culture. This last idea is essential! Failure to consider the risks created by a toxic or overly bureaucratic culture results in a weakness that threat actors can exploit.

An organization must consider cybersecurity beyond merely delegating it to technical departments. Instead, it is crucial in orchestrating DBRM. It ensures that digital business value is created, protected, and delivered securely, safeguarding the essence of organizational digital intent. Relegating cybersecurity to information technology (IT) is akin to muting a crucial instrument in a symphony, jeopardizing the harmony and, ultimately, the success of organizational performance.

Culture plays an important role in expressing strategy-risk: culture must be aligned to properly express the organizational worldview of creating, protecting, and delivering digital business value.

3.2.3　Curate your culture

Continuing with our music analogy, leaders in the digital business world are like maestros in a symphony. They have the power to shape the music of their organization not only through big declarations but also through the subtle notes of culture. When the organizational culture is in harmony with the imperative of creating, protecting, and delivering digital business value, it becomes a powerful tool for success in a constantly changing world. However, to master this orchestra of human minds and behaviors, leaders must understand their role as curators of culture and utilize the DVMS CPD Model as a tool for continual innovation.

Organizational culture is often at odds with the imperative of continuing professional development. Silos dominate, limiting the flow of information and hindering risk management. A culture of blame discourages the lifeblood of innovation: experimentation. Furthermore, leaders are often detached from the daily activities and rhythm, and fail to embody the advocated values, creating cognitive dissonance. This forces the "orchestra" to struggle, with each instrument (individual or department) playing a slightly different tune, unaware of the score, the strategic and operational intent.

Leaders must actively and continually strive to align all behaviors, values, and activities with appropriate transparency across every department. Establishing and maintaining trust, instead of the blame that discourages experimentation and learning, is also essential. Leaders must consistently demonstrate company values through their actions. In this way, they become role models rather than "speechifiers." When all these elements come together, this creates an orchestra that plays harmoniously, with every instrument contributing to the vibrant melody of sustainable digital success.

Culture constantly evolves, unlike sheet music. The DVMS CPD Model (section 2.3.2) acts as a conductor, guiding the orchestra through subtle shifts and adjustments. The model capabilities – Govern, Assure, Plan, Design, Change, Execute, and Innovate – provide the framework to:

- **Identify cultural gaps** The model helps assess how well current behaviors align with CPD objectives, highlighting areas that need improvement
- **Prioritize interventions** Not all cultural shifts have the same impact on CPD success. The model provides a way to prioritize changes based on strategy-risk
- **Experiment and iterate** Just as musicians refine their technique through practice, the model encourages small, safe experiments to test and adapt cultural interventions.

Do not expect to morph a culture via either decree or some grand overhaul plan; rather it takes a series of small and consistent adjustments that engage the staff – starting at the top. These might include implementing a new communication channel, providing training programs on risk management, or holding open-mic sessions for sharing ideas. These seemingly minor steps, when consistently repeated and combined with leaders who "walk the walk," weave a new cultural tapestry, one thread at a time. Leaders must act as curators and champion this incremental approach, nurturing trust and celebrating even the smallest wins.

Fixing a toxic or overly bureaucratic culture requires more than small adjustments. The first step should be to focus on rebuilding trust. This can be achieved through open communication, accepting responsibility, and acknowledging past mistakes. These actions should become the foundation for future progress. Only when there is a solid foundation of trust can the team or organization begin to work together toward achieving its goals.

An article by Dyer *et al.* (2023) provides valuable insights into what it takes to nurture a culture of learning and innovation. It emphasizes the delicate balance between psychological safety and open debate, both crucial elements for success. As leaders prioritize leading by example and creating a space for respectful disagreement, they pave the way for a cultural transformation beyond mere words, and show a true commitment to continuing professional development to support creating, protecting, and delivering digital business value (see also Groysberg *et al.*, 2018).

Modifying culture requires an incremental approach that starts with recognizing and acknowledging the current state, and communicating the desired changes, with leaders modeling the expected behaviors.

3.2.4   The learning organization viewed as a learning system

Let's tie a couple of ideas together. In section 2.3.2.1, we introduced a way to visualize systems thinking. We described a balancing loop (Figure 2.6) and the results of combining two balancing loops to form an escalation archetype (Figure 2.7).

Now review the CPD Model (Figure 2.5) with a focus on the two central loops – the top loop labeled "Strategy/ Governance loop" (SG loop) and the bottom loop labeled "Governance/Execution loop" (GE loop). Recall that these two loops represent an escalation archetype.

For this discussion, the SG loop provides a basis for organizational decision-making based on organizational mental models that impact strategy and governance. The GE loop provides a basis for decisions predicated on real-world experience (i.e., making tactical decisions).

The CPD Model does not provide an explicit definition of learning – or a learning organization. Nonetheless, the model's overall structure as an escalation loop provides a foundation for reconsidering the model as a representation of both a system that delivers value that is appropriately protected and a visualization of the organization as a learning system.

The model is designed to accommodate feedback from internal and external sources. The gaps in performance also potentially represent gaps in learning. We reviewed the role of questions, starting with the iceberg model (in section 2.1.1). Section 3.1.3 covered the role of questions.

Let's put these concepts together: the SG loop deals with one form of feedback impacting decisions, and the GE loop deals with another source and combines the two from the perspective of learning, and you get what is called "double-loop learning" (Wikipedia, 2024b).[26]

To put this another way, what sets the learning organization apart is using double-loop learning to evolve, not just at the tactical level, but recognizing the potential need to rethink the mental models upon which it makes decisions. We introduce the idea of leverage points in section 2.1.3. The low-order leverage points are purely tactical. The medium-order leverage points are mostly tactical, with the rudiments of strategy (i.e., the structure of information flows and system rules). The high-order leverage points can only be applied with success in a learning organization – the organization is also viewed as a learning system.

3.3 Leverage and the relationship to system structure and behavior

We introduced Donella Meadows' paper on leverage points in section 2.1.3. Here, we arrange and number them and group them from high- to low-order (lower numbers have more impact), expressed in more business-oriented terms. Remember, a small change can trigger significant, widespread effects – including unintended consequences. Think of it like identifying the location of a fulcrum for a lever: applying force at one end amplifies the movement at the other end.

High-impact:

1. **Purpose of the system (transcending paradigms in section 2.1.3)** Modifying the core justification for existence has cascading effects on goals, priorities, and all other aspects (e.g., shifting from maximizing profits to improving customer acquisition and retention with a focus on customer experience that leads to increasing the lifetime value of a customer)

2. **Mindset or paradigm** Changing the underlying assumptions and beliefs governing the system triggers widespread transformation in rules, behavior, and outcomes (e.g., transitioning from cost-cutting to growth thinking)

3. **Power to set goals and priorities** Influencing who defines system objectives and how priorities are set reshapes direction and impact (e.g., empowering marginalized organizational communities in decision-making processes)

4. **Connections between subsystems** Altering the interactions and relationships between different system parts can lead to unexpected new interactions and emergent properties (e.g., fostering cross-disciplinary collaboration – or teams – to address complex organizational challenges).

---

26 It is beyond the scope of this book to delve deeply into this topic. You can find more information about the concepts introduced in this section in an article by Nevis *et al.* (1995).

Medium-impact:

5. **Rules of the system** Modifying incentives, punishments, and constraints directly influences behaviors, shaping dynamics and outcomes (e.g., mastery-based training replacing completion)

6. **Information flow** Changing who has access to what information and how it's communicated can alter decision-making patterns and power dynamics within the system (e.g., promoting transparency and open access to data)

7. **Gain around positive feedback loops** Adjusting the amplification factors that drive growth or decline in the system can influence its overall trajectory and stability (e.g., analyze customer touchpoints and interactions to identify where small improvements will trigger positive feedback[27])

8. **Strength of negative feedback loops** Strengthening self-correcting mechanisms within the system can enhance its resilience to disruptions and promote a healthy balance (e.g., building environmental feedback loops into resource management practices).

Low-impact:

9. **Delays (response times)** Modifying the speed at which the system reacts to changes can have limited impact if the underlying causes of those changes are not addressed (e.g., build trust to push decision-making closer to the scope of effect, thus improving communication channels for faster decision-making)

10. **Material stocks and flows** Altering the physical infrastructure or resource flows may require significant effort and resources with potentially limited effects (e.g., upgrading transport networks or datacenters)

11. **Buffers and stabilizing stocks** Changing reserves or stabilizing mechanisms may offer temporary relief but won't address the root causes of system imbalances (e.g., increasing financial reserves without tackling underlying economic pressures)

12. **Numbers (constants, parameters)** Directly modifying specific numerical values like birth rates or interest rates can be a blunt tool with unpredictable and potentially unintended consequences (e.g., mandating that incident tickets must be closed within a defined period versus focusing on restoring an accepted level of productivity within a defined period).

Remember, the most impactful interventions target fundamental aspects of the system, while lower-level points offer more limited, often temporary, effects. Focusing on higher-order leverage points achieves more significant and lasting change in complex systems.

It is crucial to recognize what happens if opportunities to learn are missed, i.e., when the organization fails to apply the appropriate leverage when needed. The Fortune 500 list serves as a prime example. Every addition of a new company to the list implies that another company has been removed. According to the American Enterprise Institute (Perry, 2019), only 52 companies from the first Fortune 500 list in 1955 still were on the list in 2019. Furthermore, 89% of the companies from the 1955 list either have declared bankruptcy, have merged with or been acquired by another company, or still exist but no longer receive enough revenue to qualify for a position on the list.

Why? Because there's constant marketplace disruption. For example, IBM survived while other computer companies did not (e.g., Digital Equipment Corporation). We contend that one of the reasons why organizations are still on the list is that they figured out how to learn, adapt, and adjust to be able to thrive in the face of disruption.

---

27   The idea of understanding customer interaction points is not new to us. Steve Jobs often took customer service calls that drove changes at Apple (and occasionally at AT&T), as reported by Milian (2011).

3.3.1   Coaxing system adaptation

It is important to remember that using system leverage points has some limitations: it can take time for the system to absorb and respond, which means applying leverage may not have an immediate effect. This is especially true if unintended consequences don't have an obvious temporal cause-and-effect link. Moreover, it may be necessary to address human factors before applying the leverage (such as communicating a rule change and asking for feedback before implementing it). Both factors can introduce latency in the change process, making it difficult to correctly associate any side effects with the actual cause of the change.

The application of leverage depends on understanding the perceived current system state. The use of the word "perceived" is an essential consideration here. Different stakeholders may (and very often will) hold divergent views regarding the need for change, which makes it important to understand the expectations for goals and resulting gaps.

For these and other reasons, in section 2.1.3, we suggested that "You don't 'fix' a CAS" because, as Meadows suggested, there's no magic bullet: coaxing a CAS requires work.

3.3.2   Leverage and the four aspects of innovation

In the introduction to Chapter 2 we described the four aspects of innovation, repeated here for easy reference:

- **Incremental** innovations make small changes. In software development, this is analogous to a "point" release (e.g., version 3.1 to 3.2)
- **Sustaining** innovations are more significant. To stay with the software development analogy, sustaining innovations are a major release (e.g., version 3.2 to 4)
- **Adaptive** innovations make changes to policy
- **Disruptive** innovations result in changes to strategy.

There is a direct correlation between these innovation aspects and coaxing changes in a CAS. Figure 2.5 introduced a part of the DVMS CPD Model called the "Governance/Execution loop." This loop is where the low-order leverage points are applied in the context of incremental and sustaining innovation.

Figure 2.11 introduced the innovation and assurance part of the CPD Model. This part of the model presents the application of medium-order leverage points, including sustaining and adaptive innovations.

Finally, Figure 2.12 widens the coverage of Figure 2.10 to include the entirety of the Strategy/Governance loop, which also applies to adaptive and disruptive innovations.

To put this in a broader context, the DVMS approach suggests using innovation to coax a CAS to change – linking the concept of potentially abstract leverage points to something concrete in the context of innovation.

When viewed from the perspective of the whole DVMS CPD Model (Figure 2.5), it's critical to note the flows within the model. It includes bidirectional interactions,[28] potentially providing some feedback on the progress of applying leverage.

---

28   There's more about this idea of bidirectional relationships in the discussion about the MVC capabilities and relationships in section 3.5.2.

3.4   Continual innovation and self-organization

"Any group of people working and collaborating to reach a common goal is smarter than any single member."
David Moskowitz

Adapting and self-organizing are critical for any organization seeking to thrive. This requires agile (as in adaptive and quick to respond, not a specific agile method or approach) processes and a potent blend of individual and team mastery combined with continual innovation and adaptive work approaches. This section explores how these elements create a virtuous cycle, empowering the organization to navigate risk and achieve its objectives.

Traditional hierarchical structures often hinder agility and goal-seeking behavior. Adaptive working, on the other hand, dismantles silos, fosters cross-functional collaboration, and empowers individuals to take ownership – particularly within the context of the 3D Knowledge Model introduced in section 2.2.3 (Figure 2.4). This dynamic environment nurtures continual learning and experimentation, propelling individuals and teams toward shared goals.

In his seminal work *The Fifth Discipline*, Peter Senge outlines five "disciplines" for building a learning organization, which we briefly mentioned in section 2.4.2. Two pillars are individual and team mastery (Senge called these "personal mastery" and "team learning"). Mastery, in this context, transcends technical skills to encompass continual learning, critical thinking, and the ability to collaborate effectively within a larger purpose. When individuals and teams cultivate these qualities, they become adept at navigating complex challenges and driving innovation to achieve evolving organizational goals.

The virtuous growth cycle and experimentation can only happen in the right environment. This brings us back to the role of leadership in cultivating an adaptive, supportive, and generative culture. When leaders prioritize transparency, open communication, and risk-taking, it creates an ideal space for growth. This type of leadership encourages diverse perspectives, empowers teams to learn from their mistakes, and celebrates continual improvement.

In other words, a generative culture is the catalyst for continual innovation. As individuals and teams experience the power of collaboration and empowered decision-making, they become intrinsically motivated to seek improvements and solutions, resulting in an environment where new ideas are always encouraged, creating a vibrant ecosystem of ideas where innovation becomes the norm rather than the exception.

Innovation isn't just about flashy ideas: it's about leveraging knowledge and resources to solve problems that create and deliver appropriately protected value. This aligns perfectly with Senge's mental models discipline. By challenging outdated assumptions and embracing new perspectives, an organization unlocks a powerful lever for innovation. This, in turn, fuels the cycle of continual improvement, enabling teams to tackle unforeseen challenges and achieve developing organizational goals.

The DVMS CPD Model, focused on the creation, protection, and delivery of digital business value, provides a practical framework to apply these principles. By integrating continual personal development within an adaptive working environment, the model fosters individual and team mastery. This, coupled with a culture of innovation led by adaptive leadership, creates an organization capable of effectively self-organizing to navigate digital business risk.

Continual innovation, fueled by adaptive working, individual and team mastery, and a culture of adaptation, empowers organizations to self-organize and thrive in the face of digital business risk. By embracing Senge's principles and leveraging tools like the DVMS CPD Model, they can unlock staff potential and navigate the digital age's turbulent landscape with confidence and agility.

3.4.1 Connecting the dots

We use the term "self-organization" to refer to the ability of an organization to adapt and adjust to dynamic situations without the need for centralized control. A self-organizing organization continually adapts through the four aspects of innovation.

We suggest that continual innovation, fostered by factors like adaptive working, individual and team mastery, and a culture of adaptation, creates the conditions for self-organization. These elements empower individuals and teams to make informed decisions, share information freely, and collaborate effectively, allowing the organization to respond organically to challenges and opportunities.

Think of it this way: innovation fuels learning and growth, leading to individual and team mastery. This, combined with a supportive culture, empowers people to take ownership and solve problems collaboratively. As a result, the organization becomes fluid and dynamic, able to adjust its course without needing rigid top-down directives. This is the essence of self-organization.

High-performing teams require self-organization. This idea requires leaders to accept the responsibility for curating a multifaceted learning organization, going beyond traditional top-down command and control. There are three aspects to this responsibility:

- **Create the foundation** An adaptive and learning culture requires transparency, open communication, and acceptable risk-taking to empower individuals and teams to make decisions, experiment, and learn. This requires dismantling silos and replacing them with flexible work arrangements and cross-functional collaboration (including investing in supporting tools). The goal is to create an environment where people can effortlessly connect, share information, and get and act on feedback to work toward shared goals

- **Guide the process** Leaders must be able to act as both coach and facilitator to support team goal setting, identifying challenges and solutions – constructively, without dictating a solution. This requires the leader to connect the dots for the teams so that they understand how their efforts are aligned with and contribute to the strategic and operational intent. It also means that part of the leader's responsibility is to remove structural or procedural impediments that hinder team self-organization [29]

- **Sustain and nurture achievement** Leaders must celebrate success, period, full stop. This also applies to creating a new attitude about failure. Consider the quotation attributed to Thomas Edison regarding the invention of the lightbulb. When asked how he could persist despite 1,000 failures, he replied, "I didn't fail 1,000 times. I had 1,000 opportunities to learn what wouldn't work."[30] Seek to understand and celebrate learning, not just "success." Encourage open communication about mistakes as the source to help everyone learn. Ensure leaders and team members provide constructive feedback (rather than finger-pointing and blame) to refine the systems to support self-organization continually. A leader can only do this by example, demonstrating a personal commitment to these principles.

The leader's responsibility is to create and support the conditions for self-organization to thrive by focusing on building a culture of trust, empowerment, and continual learning. This is exactly what Microsoft CEO Satya Nadella did and meant when he wrote, "I have come to understand that my primary job is to curate our culture so that one hundred thousand inspired minds – Microsoft's employees – can better shape our future" (Nadella, 2017).

The ideas in this section (actually, the book) represent a journey, not a destination. Everything we've discussed (and will in the rest of the book) requires accepting the need for patience to coax a system to change. Use the DVMS FastTrack approach (introduced in section 2.4.1), with the understanding that FastTrack is not about time as much as it is small, incremental, manageable steps that occur within phases that make progress toward the goal.

---

29 For some, this "guide the process" comment may be reminiscent of the documented servant-leader role of the Scrum Master – a concept not limited to a particular approach or method.

30 There are several versions of this quotation. This is the one we happen to like the best.

3.4.2   Individual and team mastery

In today's world, being agile and highly adaptive is no longer a competitive advantage: it's a prerequisite. Organizations need to adopt a different mindset that enables them to create, protect, and deliver digital business value – notice, create *and* protect, not create *then* protect – while navigating the constantly changing internal and external environments.

This idea of "creating and protecting" goes beyond technology or individual training: it's a systemic approach to fostering a culture of continual learning and improvement. This culture equips individuals and teams with the skills and knowledge needed to identify the leverage points within the organizational system where appropriate interventions trigger cascading changes in behavior and outcomes.

The four aspects of innovation, combined with the phased DVMS FastTrack approach, fuel agility and adaptation by allowing an organization to experiment with new ideas and methods. By applying leverage points in a holistic "create and protect" view, teams can rapidly prototype and implement innovative solutions that better adapt to stakeholder needs and external pressure. For instance, facing regulatory changes, an organization might leverage data analytics expertise to create and deploy AI-powered compliance tools, swiftly adjusting its practices (and resulting processes) to meet new requirements.

While critical, it is insufficient to focus only on working to deliver the outcomes from a system – what we call working *in* the system. It is also essential to work *on* the system, innovating the capabilities that enable the organization to deliver the expected outcomes. Working *on* the system requires individuals and teams to demonstrate abilities in technical skills, critical thinking, collaboration, and systems thinking. When applied collectively, these abilities enable them to identify performance gaps and improve the system. We label an organization that exhibits the ability to work *on* and *in* the system simultaneously as "ambidextrous."

In his book *Out of the Crisis*, W. Edwards Deming states it directly: "Any substantial improvement must come from action on the system, the responsibility of management" (Deming, 1982). Today, we have a minor disagreement with the last phrase in the quotation. While it might be the province of management to authorize changes to the system, everyone is responsible for recognizing their role in surfacing and contributing to the actions Deming suggests.

The DVMS approach helps organizations adapt internally by promoting a shared understanding of goals. They achieve this by aligning individual and team objectives with the overall organizational vision through collaborative workshops and shared learning experiences. The 3D Knowledge Model is used to break down silos and encourage a sense of collective purpose. With this approach, individuals are able to recognize how their work contributes to the bigger picture, leading to a more coordinated and effective response to internal challenges. This is all supported and modeled by leadership.

When viewed through this holistic lens, creating, protecting, and delivering digital business value goes beyond individual training and mastery. While a culture of continual learning and improvement is essential, it's equally crucial to empower both full-time and part-time staff to embrace the principle of "If you see something, say something." This ensures the message receives a prompt response devoid of blame or neglect, a concept integrated into the Assure capability in the CPD Model.

Organizational culture profoundly influences the ability to create, protect, and deliver digital business value. A culture of trust, open communication, and risk-taking encourages individuals and teams to share ideas, experiment, and learn from mistakes. This fosters a dynamic environment where mastery flourishes and self-organization becomes possible.

3.5 Explore the MVC

The aspect of the DVMS that we call the minimum viable capabilities (MVC) represents a different way of thinking about what an organization does and how it does it. We designed the MVC as part of an overlay – meaning that everything any organization of any size does falls into one or more of the capabilities, introduced in section 1.1 (and repeated at the beginning of this chapter):

- Govern
- Assure
- Plan
- Design
- Change
- Execute
- Innovate.

Each of the seven capabilities includes one or more practice areas that aggregate related practices (see Appendix A). Each practice defines a set of outcomes that form the basis for the organization to create the processes, tasks, and activities that deliver value. This way, the DVMS overlay approach easily accommodates environmental changes, including the threat landscape and artificial intelligence.

The seven capabilities are not siloed: they are interdependent. Consider that the Plan capability is used to bootstrap the Govern and Assure capabilities. Continuing with this idea, effective governance enables adaptive planning, while continual assurance contributes to both creating and protecting digital business value.

3.5.1 The MVC as a mental model

Adopting the MVC as a mental model offers several advantages, including:

- A generative culture empowers individuals to learn and experiment; the set of MVC, treated as a mental model combined with the 3D Knowledge Model (see section 2.2.3), unlocks the potential of individuals and teams to drive innovation and growth
- The emphasis on agility and adaptivity allows an organization to navigate turbulence and remain relevant in rapidly changing environments
- Using the MVC to create and protect value creation enables efficient and effective execution by minimizing the waste and associated downtime to "fix it later," thus ensuring that the organization thrives.

The 3D Knowledge Model is an aspect of the application of the MVC. Consider Figure 2.4, which represents a single team and its interactions. With more than one team, it's possible to "stack" the model, as shown in Figure 3.1. When the planes in the model form a vertical cylinder, the culture is aligned throughout the organization. However, if the lines are not vertically aligned (i.e., they are off kilter) – in other words, different teams in the stack operate differently with varying degrees of siloed activities – this indicates a need for leadership to address cultural alignment.

3.5.2 MVC (Z-X Model) capabilities and relationships

The minimum viable capabilities, as noted above, are interdependent.[31] This concept is one of the ideas behind why we say that everything the organization is already doing maps to one or more of these capabilities. One way of illustrating this is shown in Figure 3.4, which includes the heptagon border as the connection to the adjacent capability.

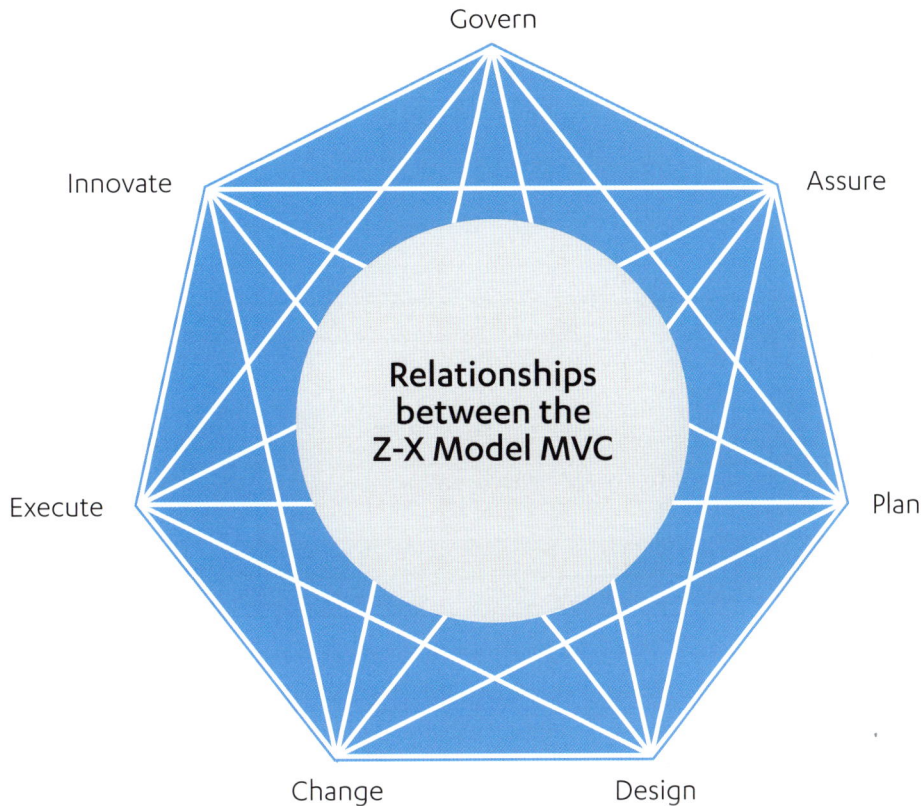

Govern

Innovate

Assure

Relationships between the Z-X Model MVC

Execute

Plan

Change

Design

Figure 3.4 Each capability is related to the other six

If we decompose this to the practice area level (see Appendix A) and provide names for the practice areas associated with Plan, Design, Change, Execute, and Innovate, we get Table 3.1.

---

31   As noted in section 2.3.3, we use the terms "MVC" and "Z-X Model" interchangeably.

Table 3.1 MVC relationships

DVMS practice areas	PL: Governance	PL: Assurance	PL: Strategy-risk management	PL: Portfolio, program, and project management	PL: Knowledge management	DE: System architecture	DE: Configuration management	CH: Change coordination	CH: Solution adaptation	CH: Release management	CH: Deployment management	EX: Provisioning	EX: Productivity management	EX: Problem management	EX: Infrastructure/platform management	IN: Continual innovation	IN: Performance measurement	IN: Gap analysis
PL: Governance	-	B	B	B	B	B	-	B	-	-	-	-	-	-	-	B	B	B
PL: Assurance	B	-	B	B	B	B	-	T	-	-	-	-	-	-	-	B	T	B
PL: Strategy-risk management	B	B	-	B	B	B	B	T	T	T	T	-	-	-	-	B	T	B
PL: Portfolio, program, and project management	B	B	B	-	B	B	-	T	-	-	-	-	-	-	-	B	T	B
PL: Knowledge management	B	B	B	B	-	B	B	B	B	B	B	B	B	B	B	B	B	B
DE: System architecture	B	B	B	B	B	-	B	B	F	-	-	-	-	-	-	B	B	B
DE: Configuration management	-	-	B	-	B	B	-	T	B	T	T	-	T	T	T	B	B	B
CH: Change coordination	B	F	F	F	B	B	B	-	B	B	B	-	-	-	-	B	B	B
CH: Solution adaptation	-	-	F	-	B	-	B	B	-	F	F	-	-	-	-	B	B	B
CH: Release management	-	-	F	-	B	-	F	B	T	-	T	-	-	-	-	B	B	B
CH: Deployment management	-	-	F	-	B	-	F	B	T	F	-	-	-	-	-	B	B	B
EX: Provisioning	-	-	-	-	B	-	-	-	-	-	-	-	F	F	T	B	B	B
EX: Productivity management	-	-	-	-	B	-	F	-	-	-	-	T	-	B	T	B	B	B
EX: Problem management	-	-	-	-	B	-	F	-	-	-	-	T	B	-	T	B	B	B
EX: Infrastructure/platform management	-	-	-	-	B	-	F	-	-	-	-	F	F	F	-	B	B	B
IN: Continual innovation	B	F	F	F	B	B	B	B	B	B	B	B	B	B	B	-	B	B
IN: Performance measurement	B	B	B	B	B	B	B	B	B	B	B	B	B	B	B	B	-	B
IN: Gap analysis	B	B	B	B	B	B	B	B	B	B	B	B	B	B	B	B	B	-

Key to practice areas

■ Plan capability   ■ Design capability   ■ Change capability   ■ Execute capability   ■ Innovate capability

We have omitted the Govern and Assure capabilities from the table because they have a bidirectional relationship with every other capability; adding them would clutter the table needlessly.

This interdependence between capabilities supports the idea of desiloization – breaking down silos.

3.6   Chapter takeaways

One of the primary ideas expressed in this chapter is related to the concept of systems thinking introduced in Chapter 2. Specifically, not only should the organization be viewed in the context of a system – it is, at the same time, a learning system.

Recognizing and adapting mental models is based on feedback derived from learning. The same thing is true regarding cultural adaptation. One of the new mental models requires reframing or reimagining strategy and risk as a single entity, strategy-risk, instead of treating them separately. The first set of questions in QO–QM requires input from strategy-risk.

Coaxing system changes requires understanding leverage points – with the understanding that the higher the impact, the longer it might take before the anticipated adaptation is realized.

The 3D Knowledge Model provides an example of intra- and inter-team coordination, communication, and collaboration; it also provides a learning model and a context to ask different and/or better questions. Besides being a "knowledge model," it is also a cultural model (as you'll see in Chapter 4).

The final takeaway from this chapter is the idea that everything is connected. The MVC (Govern, Assure, Plan, Design, Change, Execute, and Innovate) are related and depend on each other – this is consistent with the idea of a system.

CHAPTER 4
Leadership, accountability, and culture

4 Leadership, accountability, and culture

"The strength of the team is each individual member.
The strength of each member is the team."
Phil Jackson

The opening quotation from Phil Jackson, head coach of multiple National Basketball Association (NBA) teams with 11 NBA titles to his credit, highlights the interdependence of individual team members and the entirety of the team. Extending this idea, the whole organization depends on the collective behaviors of its members – everyone in the organization, from the top down.

In today's fast-paced and ever-changing business environment, leaders must acknowledge their critical role in shaping organizational (team) culture. It's not enough for them to be the coach in the Phil Jackson sense: they must cultivate an environment that encourages continual learning, agility, and resilience. This is especially important in a CAS,[32] where outcomes may not be immediately obvious.

4.1   A learning organization is an adaptive organization

The foundation of the adaptive organization is built on an adaptive culture that encourages learning (from successes and failures), collaboration, and experimentation. At its core, this culture enables and promotes critical thinking, challenges assumptions, and nudges people to explore outside their comfort zones. However, such a culture requires deliberate creation and continual attention. The accountability and responsibility to curate this type of culture falls squarely on the shoulders of leadership – starting with the highest-level individual: the CEO or equivalent.

Leaders set the tone and expectations through words, actions, and decisions. Like it or not, leaders are role models shaping expectations and influencing behaviors. By prioritizing transparency, open communication, and psychological safety, they create a platform for genuine collaboration and knowledge sharing. Additionally, actively seeking diverse perspectives and encouraging experimentation cultivates a culture of continual learning, which is critical to navigating the complexities of modern business.

These characteristics are fundamental to developing an organizational mindset focusing on creating and *concurrently* protecting, rather than creating and *serially* protecting digital business value. This is true whether the discussion is about the threat landscape or the influence and impact of artificial intelligence (also used by threat actors). The idea is that it's essential to develop a holistic, "systems-based" view of the world to see the bigger picture – making it more likely to solve problems instead of treating symptoms.

---

32   You might suggest that your organization isn't complex, because it has only a few people. However, the term "complex adaptive system" is used in a broader context to include the entire ecosystem in which your organization exists.

4.1.1 The 3D Knowledge Model and collaboration

The 3D Knowledge Model (see section 2.2.3 and Figure 2.4) offers a valuable framework to visualize and understand the flow of knowledge and work within a team, between teams, and in the organization. Each team member must understand and apply an organizational interpretation of the three axes to gain deeper insights into how knowledge interacts with and influences various aspects of work.

The following description is deliberately written from an individual's perspective:

- First, place the initial focus on "my" team (the X-axis) by ensuring you know (and each member knows) and appreciate knowledge about your past, present, and future activities. This reflects a strong grasp of internal awareness, a crucial component of any successful team. Knowing what you've done, what you're currently doing, and what lies ahead on the horizon equips your team with a solid foundation to plan, adapt, and achieve goals

- Second, build awareness of the Y-axis and its emphasis on the interconnectedness within the organization. Using this axis appropriately recognizes how other teams affect your team and vice versa, fostering a collaborative mindset that encourages proactive communication. By anticipating the impact of your actions on others while being attuned to their influences, your team can navigate interdependencies effectively, ensuring smooth operations and optimized outcomes

- Finally, work to understand how the Z-axis positions strategic and operational intent at the core of knowledge flow. This highlights the importance of aligning your team's work with the bigger picture. By integrating a clear understanding of strategic goals and operational objectives into your activities, your team can ensure its efforts contribute meaningfully to the overall organizational success.

It is essential to note that using the term "team" in the above points applies to every organizational team, starting with the highest executive team and cascading to every other team. This means that the scope of application of the Y- and Z-axes changes at each organizational level. How does a decision made by "this" team impact every other team – something essential for the highest executive team to consider?

Now, let's connect this to the bigger picture regarding each axis and organizational behavior, structure, and leadership: [33]

- **X-axis** Represents the behavioral norms and values within the system, reflecting intra-team awareness and collaboration
- **Y-axis** Captures the organizational structure expressed as the formal and informal networks and relationships, connecting to understanding interdependencies
- **Z-axis** Encompasses the leadership expression of vision, direction, and decision-making that guides the system, mirroring the emphasis on strategic and operational intent.

Taken as a whole, an evaluation of these two explanations of the 3D Knowledge Model, combined with the discussion of the cultural web in section 2.2 and the discussion relating the model to culture in section 3.1.2, provides insight into how to morph and curate organizational culture.

By embracing this integrated view of knowledge, you can leverage the 3D Knowledge Model to:

- **Break down silos** Share knowledge across the axes, fostering better collaboration and understanding
- **Identify gaps and opportunities** Analyze knowledge distribution and utilization to optimize workflows and decision-making
- **Promote continual learning** Encourage knowledge sharing, and encourage individuals to learn across all axes
- **Strengthen teamwork** Cultivate a shared ownership and responsibility culture by understanding dependencies and strategic goals.

---

33   We introduced this idea in section 3.1.2 and in the discussion of Figure 3.1.

Leading in a CAS requires a shift from fixed mindsets to adaptive cultures. An organization can cultivate an environment where continual learning, collaboration, and risk awareness blossom by understanding the intricate interplay between leadership, accountability, and culture, and by leveraging frameworks like the 3D Knowledge Model and the DVMS CPD Model. This fertile ground allows the organization to create and protect value effectively, navigating the ever-changing business landscape.

4.1.2   The DVMS CPD Model and a learning organization

We discussed the DVMS CPD Model[34] in Chapter 2 (see Figure 2.5), with a focus on creating, protecting, and delivering digital business value that seamlessly aligns with the goals of an adaptive culture. The feedback loops in the model emphasize continual learning and development; the model equips individuals and teams in the organization with the skills and knowledge necessary to navigate an ever-evolving landscape with an ongoing appreciation of performance gaps. The model fosters a shared understanding of risk (strategy-risk), empowering individuals to identify and address potential issues proactively.

Organizations constantly grapple with creating, protecting, and delivering value amid ever-changing landscapes. The CPD Model, a systems escalation archetype (see section 2.3.2.1 and Figure 2.7), emerges as a valuable framework for navigating this complexity. It provides a unique blend of strategy, governance, and execution while emphasizing the crucial role of adaptation in ensuring long-term success.

To keep things simple, we focus on five aspects of the model:

- Strategy/Governance loop:

  - **Create** This loop focuses on developing the vision and roadmap for digital business initiatives. Depending on organizational resources, it may involve market research, competitor analysis, and technology exploration (e.g., to identify high-potential opportunities)

  - **Protect** This phase emphasizes setting up the necessary governance structures and frameworks to guide decision-making, manage risks, and ensure regulatory compliance, along with the framework to concurrently protect value creation

- Governance/Execution loop:

  - **Protect** This loop reiterates the importance of ongoing governance throughout the execution phase. It entails monitoring progress, measuring performance, and mitigating emerging risks

  - **Deliver** This stage brings the strategy to life, focusing on implementation, operational excellence, and delivering tangible value to customers

- The outer right-side arc that flows through "QO–QM":

  - Combines "create," "protect," and "deliver" to ensure that the value created is appropriately protected and can be delivered. This idea requires that implementors who create value work with auditors who ensure value is appropriately protected – and, depending on the circumstances, potentially also with people charged with value delivery – to develop the two sets of questions: first to validate the outcomes from these perspectives, and second to ensure monitoring, measuring, and metric collection and analysis are consistent with the first set

---

34 The terms "create" and "protect" do not explicitly appear in the model – it is the totality of what an organization does to achieve this goal. Creating and protecting value starts with strategy-risk and cascades throughout the model. See sections 2.3.2.3 and 3.1.5.3 for the discussions about implementors and auditors collaborating to create and protect value.

- The left-side arc through "Assure":

  · Combines the three aspects of CPD to ensure that the value delivered meets stakeholder expectations (current and evolving) and includes appropriate protection

- "Adapt" – the bridge:

  · The true power of the CPD Model lies in the connection through "Adapt," which acts as the crucial bridge, ensuring agility and responsiveness in a dynamic environment. Every organization that uses this model starts at the same place: at "Adapt"

  · Adapt "Strategy" as a response to disruptive innovation: Based on insights from the Execute and Govern capabilities, adjust and refine the initial strategy to reflect market shifts, competitor actions, or unforeseen challenges

  · Adapt "Govern" responding to an adaptive innovation – the Govern capability develops policy: As the initiative evolves, governance frameworks may need to be adapted to maintain effectiveness and responsiveness

  This is the entry point, for every organization, to the model: start where you are and adapt.

By adopting the CPD Model, an organization reaps several benefits:

- **Holistic approach** It encompasses the entire value chain, from identifying opportunities to delivering value, offering a comprehensive perspective
- **Risk management** The emphasis on governance in both loops ensures strategic risks are identified and mitigated proactively – the essence of strategy-risk
- **Agility and adaptability** The model promotes continual learning and adaptation, allowing the organization to respond swiftly to changing conditions
- **Alignment and focus** The interconnectedness fosters alignment between strategy, governance, and execution, ensuring everyone works toward shared goals.

Implementing the CPD Model requires careful consideration of several factors:

- **Define clear roles and responsibilities** Clearly define who owns each stage of the loops and how collaboration occurs between them
- **Establish effective communication** Ensure seamless communication across functions and teams to facilitate information sharing and adaptation
- **Leverage technology** Utilize technology tools and platforms to support data-driven decision-making, risk management, and performance monitoring
- **Foster a culture of learning** Curate a culture that embraces experimentation, feedback, and continual improvement to drive adaptation.

The CPD Model offers a valuable overlay approach for navigating the complexities of creating and protecting digital business value. Understanding the interconnected loops and emphasizing organizational adaptation enables the organization to meet evolving needs, scale effectively, unlock agility, build resilience, and thrive in the ever-evolving digital landscape. Whether your organization is just starting its digital journey or seeking to optimize existing initiatives, embracing the CPD Model can be a transformative step toward creating, protecting, and delivering sustainable digital business value.

4.2   Leadership, accountability, and oversight

"The ability to learn is the most important quality a leader can have."
Padmasree Warrior

In any successful organization, three critical elements function together that enable it to achieve its desired outcomes: leadership, accountability, and oversight. Each plays a distinct role, yet they are intricately interconnected, forming the backbone of a well-governed system.

Effective **leadership** goes beyond inspiring words: it demands a clear understanding of roles, relationships, and accountability. Leaders must provide clear direction and expectations while empowering teams to make decisions and take action. Clear reporting structures and accountability mechanisms ensure everyone understands their role and contribution to goals.

Picture a team collaborating on a project. Everyone has a specific role, set responsibilities, and clear relationships with others. In the same way, organizational roles and relationships determine how leadership and accountability function. The board of directors, acting as the ultimate responsible entity, establishes the strategic direction and holds the executive team accountable for achieving stated objectives.[35] This **accountability** guarantees consistency between vision and action. Clear reporting structures and communication channels further reinforce this connection, providing a framework for decision-making and performance evaluation.

Oversight acts as the strategic advisor in this scenario. It goes beyond simply observing, encompassing two distinct yet complementary functionalities: active guidance and informed evaluation.

Active guidance involves monitoring performance, proactively identifying potential issues, and suggesting corrective actions as innovations, providing timely insights and adjustments to keep things on track.

Oversight in this context is crucial; it is an essential aspect of both leadership and accountability. Oversight provides two main functions: active guidance and informed evaluation. Active guidance involves monitoring and improving performance by identifying and addressing potential issues sooner. Informed evaluation provides data-driven insights and metrics, facilitated by the QO–QM (see sections 3.1.4 and 3.1.5 and subsections). This involves both implementors, who generate value, and auditors, who determine whether the value is appropriately protected. Together, they work from ideation to delivery, enabling proactive adjustments to achieve organizational goals.

So that there is no doubt, let's define the core terms:

- **Leadership** The ability to influence and inspire individuals to achieve a common goal, going beyond the current state and embracing progress
- **Accountability** The obligation to answer for one's actions and performance, ensuring alignment with agreed objectives and goals
- **Oversight** The act of monitoring, guiding, and influencing organizational performance, encompassing active intervention and insightful analysis.

Leadership, accountability, and oversight form a powerful triumvirate, guiding an organization toward success. Understanding their distinct roles, relationships, and nuances within the MVC framework sets the stage for further exploration.

---

35   Note: the board of directors, executive team, etc., are roles. While there may be only a small number of people in the organization, someone still provides one of more of these functions.

4.2.1   Ensuring a common understanding of leader and manager roles

Although the two terms are often used interchangeably, the differences between leadership and management are crucial. In the context of the MVC, a set of seven essential organizational capabilities (see Chapter 2), this distinction becomes even more apparent.

Leadership is the driving force behind any successful organization:

- Creating a vision that inspires individuals to work toward ambitious goals
- Fostering a culture of continual learning and adaptation, which in turn leads to positive change within the organization. This requires that leaders establish expectations and serve as the model for the desired behaviors (in and outside of the office)
- Within the MVC: participating in capabilities such as planning and innovation
- Outside of the MVC: visionary thinking, strategic planning, and emotional intelligence.

Management focuses on ensuring that daily operations run smoothly and that objectives are met:

- Focusing on execution with day-to-day operational responsibilities
- Translating strategic goals into actionable plans
- Allocating resources, and ensuring that they are utilized efficiently and effectively in alignment with governance and assurance – holding people accountable as necessary
- Delegating responsibilities
- Operating within the MVC framework.

Key differences:

- **Focus** Managers focus on tasks and processes, while leaders focus on people and vision
- **Approach** Managers prioritize stability and order, while leaders champion change and innovation
- **Skills** Managers excel in organization and execution, while leaders excel in inspiration and motivation.

While distinct, these roles are not mutually exclusive. Effective managers often display leadership qualities, and strong leaders need management skills to translate vision into reality. The ultimate goal is to achieve a healthy balance between the two, ensuring efficient execution and forward-thinking direction.

Both managers and leaders play crucial roles in ensuring the success of an organization. While managers drive daily operations and accountability, leaders provide the vision and inspiration to move forward. Understanding these distinct roles and fostering collaboration leads to a thriving and adaptable organization.

4.2.2   Leadership and accountability

The concepts of leadership and accountability, previously discussed in this chapter, require a clear understanding of navigating the complexities of digital business risk. There are distinct roles for the board and leaders in an organization, and these require examining their responsibilities and suggesting approaches for effectively managing digital business risk.

This idea starts with the principle that there cannot be lines between strategy and risk. We introduced the idea of strategy-risk as a single entity in section 2.1. Today, it is essential that the idea of strategy-risk takes supremacy over two different organizational "departments." Strategy-risk demands seamless integration of risk considerations into the fabric of strategic decision-making and everything that flows from it. This necessitates rethinking leadership and accountability for a world where navigating complexity and embracing calculated risks are key to survival and success.

Gone are the days of separate domains for strategy and risk. The board, acting as the ultimate guardian of value, bears the responsibility for guiding and overseeing strategy-risk integration, which translates to:

- **Defining the risk appetite** Establish a clear framework for acceptable risk levels within strategic goals applied to organizational decision-making
- **Challenging strategic assumptions** Develop questions based on a risk-informed strategy for all proposed initiatives as part of QO–QM (see sections 2.3.2.3 and 3.1.3). The object is to identify and address potential risk-related pitfalls sooner – at the beginning, not at the end
- **Holding leaders accountable** Demand robust risk assessments, effective mitigation strategies, and transparent communication throughout the strategic journey.

These ideas suggest a change in how the organization typically views strategy and risk as separate entities (department or views). This approach creates an inherent tension because strategy and risk are treated separately. Taking a strategy-risk-based approach puts one person in the accountable position for creating and protecting value who must have sufficient information to make informed decisions. This is one of the reasons for implementors and auditors to collaborate and participate in the QO–QM activities.

To put this another way, all levels of the organization (leaders and team members) become architects of adaptive, risk-aware strategies with the following accountabilities:

- **Embedding risk awareness** Foster a culture where risk is openly discussed, understood, and integrated into every decision
- **Building dynamic strategies** Craft flexible and adaptable plans that anticipate and respond to emerging risks and opportunities
- **Communicating with clarity** Transparently articulate risk implications of strategic choices, both potential upside and downside, to stakeholders at all levels
- **Escalating proactively** Promptly raise red flags and seek guidance when significant or unexpected risks occur.

The board must trust leaders to execute a strategy-risk lens approach, while leaders must provide transparent and timely insights on risk landscapes. This idea is essential for a proactive response when early warning systems emerge – how can we turn "this concern" into an opportunity for proactive planning and mitigation, not reactive panic?

A prerequisite to enabling this proactive behavior is to ensure that informed decisions rule. Organizational resiliency demands that strategies be not only ambitious but also realistic, and include consideration for potential risks and associated impact. A by-product of this approach is that innovation thrives because calculated risk-taking becomes a part of the strategic narrative, enabling the exploration of new opportunities while managing downside potential.

Clear expectations guide both the board and leaders in this new paradigm. The board sets expectations for risk analysis, communication protocols, and risk mitigation strategies. Leaders, in turn, set expectations for their teams, ensuring everyone understands their role in identifying, assessing, and managing risks within the strategic context – think about this in the context of the 3D Knowledge Model. [36]

Effectively navigating the intertwined world of strategy-risk requires a shift in mindset resulting in different actions, which is a theme of this book. Organizational roles must evolve to accept new, potentially different responsibilities of the board, leaders, managers, and staff, emphasizing the importance of collaboration, trust, and shared accountability. Embracing this integrated approach enables the organization to establish a basis for agility and resiliency.

---

36 We haven't discussed "consequences" when the models are ignored. When expectations are unmet, there should be swift consequences that promote accountability and drive improvement.

4.2.3 Leadership and oversight

Leadership and oversight roles represent different sides of the same coin. The leadership role provides an attentive guardian, proactively managing risks and seeking opportunities. On the other hand, the oversight role involves being watchful and ensuring alignment with strategic and operational intent while enabling responsible risk-taking.

In the past, oversight was seen as passive observation. However, in today's dynamic world, a more proactive approach is necessary. Oversight goes beyond identifying issues: it involves actively investigating potential risks, questioning assumptions, and proposing mitigation strategies.

Effective oversight encourages open dialogue and teamwork among leaders, risk management teams, the board, and all staff members. This collaborative approach ensures decisions are made with a comprehensive understanding incorporating lessons from past experiences. Additionally, it allows for adapting oversight methods to tackle new and emerging risks, which is vital for maintaining sustained effectiveness.

This idea is incorporated into the CPD Model and the 3D Knowledge Model.

Oversight involves observing and seeking alignment, while leadership involves fostering a culture that integrates strategy-risk awareness into every decision, from strategic planning to daily operations. This entails establishing strong risk management frameworks, implementing effective controls, and ensuring compliance with regulations.

It is essential for leaders to continually monitor risk indicators, determine risk exposure, and provide timely and meaningful reports to stakeholders, including the board. Part of this reporting mandates promptly alerting the board and relevant stakeholders about severe risks that require immediate attention or strategic intervention. It is equally necessary for leaders to provide regular updates, both upstream and downstream, review risk reports, and take corrective actions when necessary to ensure alignment with strategic objectives and risk tolerance levels.

While leaders are critical in day-to-day oversight, ultimate accountability rests with the board. The board members function as the custodians of value, ensuring responsible management of digital business risks. The board defines the organizational risk appetite, establishes appropriate risk management frameworks, and sets clear leadership expectations. It provides strategic guidance, challenges assumptions, and provides resources to empower leaders to manage risks effectively.

Although the board holds the highest level of accountability, assigning final responsibility to the entire body dilutes accountability. Therefore, it is crucial to appoint a specific board member as the ultimate accountable individual for oversight. This person, commonly known as the oversight committee chair or risk committee chair, leads the board's risk oversight activities and serves as the main point of contact for communication and reporting.

Effective management of digital business risk requires a culture that values shared responsibility and empowers leaders with the authority and resources to make decisions based on informed strategies and risk analysis. It also requires trust in leaders to exercise sound judgment. Trust is further enhanced by open and transparent communication that encourages the exchange of information, expression of concerns, and diversity of perspectives. Information sharing and communication foster a culture of continual learning and innovation, allowing the organization to learn from successes, near misses, and failures. The ultimate goal of this approach is to promote a culture of learning and growth.

Effective leadership and oversight are central requirements to manage risks and recognize and capitalize on opportunities. Embracing the concept of watchful and responsible care, designating individual accountability within the board, and fostering a culture of shared responsibility enables the organization to navigate the digital frontiers with agility and resiliency. It provides a basis for confidence in sustained organizational success.

4.3   The risk team

Effectively managing digital business risk demands well-orchestrated collaboration within a multi-layered framework. The idea driving this approach stems from the groundwork laid in previous sections of this book – specifically, the notion that empowered diverse perspectives, underpinned by collaborative teamwork, provide a more "intelligent" approach to decision-making and resulting action than relying on a single individual.

The following discussion refers to a "risk team" that can be easily scaled. Though we use the term "risk team," it is not a formal structure; it is a shared mindset supported by transparent and open communication, as explained in sections 4.2.2 and 4.2.3. It is a multi-layered model with interactions, as illustrated in Figure 4.1.

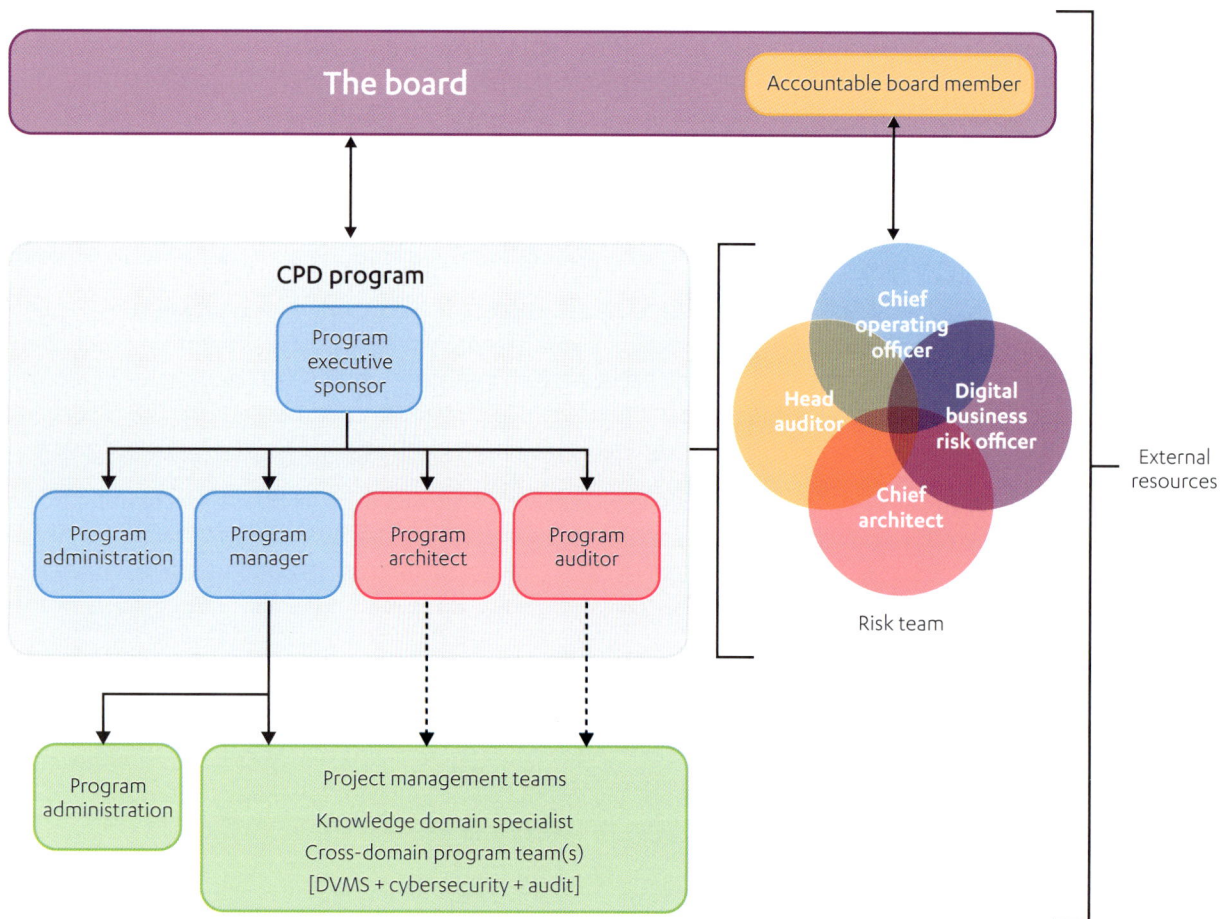

Figure 4.1 The risk team and interactions

The board represents the ultimate stewards of risk management – with one member designated as the point person, assuming direct accountability. This role covers the following responsibilities:

- Defining and publishing the organizational risk appetite, which extends to establishing risk governance frameworks and ensuring alignment with strategic objectives
- Regularly monitoring risk assessments and mitigation strategies, challenging assumptions, and offering strategic guidance to the executive team
- Holding leaders accountable by requiring regular updates, reviewing risk reports, and taking corrective actions to ensure responsible risk management.

The risk team, led by the chief operations officer (COO) or equivalent role, owns the operational responsibility to execute and manage digital business risk, which involves:

- Building a risk-aware culture, creating an environment where risk awareness permeates every decision, embedding risk management into daily operations
- Implementing risk management frameworks that provide robust processes to identify, assess, mitigate, and monitor risks across all operational areas
- Escalating critical issues by promptly informing the board and relevant stakeholders of severe risks requiring immediate attention or strategic intervention.

We introduce a new role crucial to the risk team: the digital business risk officer (DBRO). The DBRO champions digital business risk management (DBRM) inherent in strategy-risk, ensuring these considerations are at the forefront of all decisions. Some organizations may decide to convert the role of chief information security officer (CISO) or equivalent to the DBRO role, which requires a fundamental mindset change from asset protection to strategy-risk assessment and policy development.

With that as a prelude, the risk team includes the following roles:

- **The COO** oversees risk management from an operational perspective, ensuring alignment with strategic goals and efficient resource allocation
- **The DBRO** champions DBRM, developing and implementing frameworks and policies tailored to the digital landscape
- **The chief architect** (responsible for value creation) ensures that system design and technology choices consider security, robustness, and resilience, mitigating potential vulnerabilities
- **The head auditor** (responsible for overall quality, including value protection) provides independent oversight, monitoring adherence to policies, controls, and best practices, ensuring the effectiveness of risk management.

Within this framework, the risk team plays a crucial role. In this scenario, the team composition reflects an approach to risk management. This collaborative approach ensures comprehensive risk identification, assessment, and mitigation, safeguarding value creation while optimizing overall organizational performance. The architect and auditor may also be part of management teams.

A role not always associated with the management team – but essential from a systems perspective – is that of an advisor (or equivalent) to the portfolio, program, and project teams. This role is a central resource, providing guidance and support to ensure consistent risk management practices across initiatives. The person filling this role could be the program architect (as shown in Figure 4.1) or another designated individual. Note that this role is consistent with having someone responsible for ensuring appropriate communication across the Y-axis of the 3D Knowledge Model.

While defined roles ensure clarity and accountability, collaboration across layers remains essential.[37] The board relies on the risk team, via the accountable board member, for insights and updates; the risk team leverages the expertise of the chief architect, head auditor, and DBRO for informed decision-making. Effective communication and knowledge sharing between all layers also foster a wide-ranging understanding of the risk landscape and enable proactive mitigation strategies.

---

37   This includes a single layer of the 3D Knowledge Model in Figure 2.4 and the multi-layered version shown in Figure 3.1.

4.4 Chapter takeaways

A learning organization is an adaptive organization – an idea that applies to the whole enterprise, regardless of size or sector (including industry, government, academia, and nonprofits). Becoming a learning organization requires leadership responsibility to curate an appropriate culture.

The 3D Knowledge Model is polymorphic[38] in the sense that it models work flows, communication flows, and knowledge flows as well as organizational culture.

The CPD Model is an abstraction that represents how an organization creates and protects digital business value. It links the behaviors of implementors and auditors (starting with QO–QM to develop appropriate metrics – as noted in section 3.1.5.3).

The risk team may or may not be a formal body. However, its role is essential.

---

38 We use this term similarly to its usage in object-oriented programming.

CHAPTER 5
Shaping outcomes

5 Shaping outcomes

*"Experience is what you get when you didn't get what you wanted.
And experience is often the most valuable thing you have to offer."*
Randy Pausch, *The Last Lecture*

Learning and gaining experience from unexpected outcomes provides a valuable opportunity to understand your expectations and the reasoning behind them without any biases. It can be challenging to understand emergent behaviors in CAS. You need to understand system components and behaviors to achieve the desired outcomes. Instead of attempting to change the entire system, apply leverage (see section 2.1.3) at the appropriate point to align system behavior with your goals.

The Digital Value Management System overlay approach includes a set of minimum viable capabilities (MVC) represented in the DVMS Z-X Model. The CPD Model represents an organization as a CAS. These two concepts address internal and external organizational needs, and the threat landscape.

By continually innovating, adapting, and achieving the desired level of resiliency, the CPD Model enables the organization to apply the appropriate leverage to affect overall system behavior (see the discussion in sections 2.1 and 3.3). However, this requires individuals in the organization to operate with a cultural imperative to create, protect, and deliver digital business value.

When the learning organization harnesses this imperative in the context of a shared vision, it becomes self-organizing. It adapts to meet internal needs, external requirements, and a dynamic threat landscape while operating effectively.

To achieve this ideal state of a CAS, we must understand how to work *on* and *in* the system concurrently. Everything learned helps achieve this ability to adapt and operate.

5.1   Connecting the DVMS CPD Model to the DVMS Z-X Model

The CPD Model operationalizes the Z-X Model's MVC to create, protect, and deliver digital business value. Each capability describes a set of practice areas and practices that define outcomes. We introduced these models in Chapter 2: see Figures 2.5 and 2.1 respectively.

5.1.1   Operationalizing the DVMS Z-X Model

The DVMS Z-X Model represents the minimum organizational capabilities necessary to create appropriately protected digital business value. By "appropriately protected," we mean the level of protection is proportional to its value to the organization.

Recall that the DVMS overlay aspect (review Chapter 2 with a focus on section 2.3.4) defines the MVC as providing practice areas that aggregate the practices necessary to create, protect, and deliver digital business value.

The following describes the capabilities, practice areas, practices, and outcomes. The description includes any internal DVMS relationships, a maturity capability model (see Table B.1), and demonstrable artifacts for each outcome at each capability level.

5.1.2 The DVMS Model capabilities and practice areas

Chapter 2 gives a brief overview of the seven DVMS capabilities, which we call the MVC, applicable to any organization (see Figure 2.1). Everything the organization does falls into one or more of the MVC. For example, hiring involves every capability:

- **Govern** establishes appropriate personnel policies
- **Assure** establishes a verifiable need to impact organizational performance
- **Plan** ensures appropriate stakeholder communication (knowledge management)
- **Design** ensures the skills associated with the new hires are appropriately documented and considered
- **Change** ensures the new people are appropriately integrated into the environment
- **Execute** ensures these people have access to the appropriate "stuff" (provisioning)
- **Innovate** measures their performance.

Each capability represents practice areas[39] that aggregate specific practices. It is an organizational responsibility to develop the processes that implement and execute the tasks and activities associated with each practice. This approach is another way the DVMS scales by describing scalable outcomes associated with practice areas.

5.1.2.1 Govern practice areas

Govern produces organizational objectives that result in cascading management policies as tools to create the organizational capabilities to create, protect, and deliver digital business value. The board of directors sets the rules and goals for the system that is the organization. From a scalable overlay perspective, the "board of directors" represents a role, not a specific body. It is the most senior accountability role in the organization, which could be a formal several-member body or a founding individual of a startup.

This body or individual establishes the business objectives to achieve the goals. The policies provide the guidance that creates or improves the organizational capabilities to produce the desired behaviors.

At a very high level, a typical Govern set of practices addresses the following:

- Structure
  - Organizational design and reporting structure
  - Structure and charters
- Oversight responsibilities
  - Management accountability and authority
  - Committee accountability, authorities, and responsibilities
- Talent and culture
  - Performance management and incentives
  - Business and operating principles
  - Leadership development and talent programs

---

39   This chapter provides an overview of the practice areas. You'll find a detailed account in Appendix A.

- Infrastructure

    · Policies and procedures

    · Transparency in reporting and communication

    · Digital business value.

It's essential to understand that some of these areas are crafted as a part of the Plan capability (e.g., organizational design). In other words, it is critical to understand that these capabilities are not silos of activities.

5.1.2.2   Assure practice areas

The Assure capability of the DVMS/Z-X Model provides the organization with confidence in executing its strategic policies. The resultant organizational capabilities give the appropriate level of warranty and utility (fitness for use and purpose) the organization requires. While the Govern capability establishes the "what and how" the organization achieves its objectives, Assure provides "proof" that the appropriate innovation authority addresses performance gaps.

There are four practice areas:

- Establishing assurance criteria

    · Instrument warranty and utility of the DVMS capabilities

- Assuring strategic policy performance

    · Identify performance gaps in the execution of strategic policy

- Assuring operational capability

    · Identify performance gaps relative to fitness and use

- Assuring performance measurement accuracy

    · Identify gaps in the accuracy of the strategic and operational intent schema.

5.1.2.3   Plan practice areas

The Plan capability enables the organization to govern, assure performance, create and execute a risk-informed business strategy, and manage its portfolio of programs, risks, projects, and organizational knowledge. The practice areas of the Plan capability subsequently enable it to create, protect, and deliver digital business value.

The purpose of the Plan capability subsumes two goals: 1) the creation and delivery of digital business value and 2) concurrently protecting value delivered at a level commensurate with its importance to the business.

Five practice areas are part of the Plan capability:

- Governance
- Assurance
- Strategy-risk management
- Portfolio, program, and project management
- Knowledge management.

You may ask why governance and assurance appear here. The reason, as previously mentioned, is that capabilities are not silos. The Plan capability bootstraps governance and assurance.

5.1.2.4   Design practice areas

The Design capability enables the organization to take a straightforward, cohesive approach to creating, protecting, and delivering digital business value. The Design capability develops "designs" through the architecture practice area. We use the term "architecture" generically to include enterprise and system architecture and the resulting designs. The configuration management practice area provides the information necessary to perform the activities associated with the architecture practice area (including people and their skills, physical stuff, and more).

This highlights an important idea: Think of the capabilities and associated practice areas as part of the organization as a system. From this perspective, planning (as a capability) is involved in every practice area across all capabilities.

Practice areas:

- System architecture
- Configuration management.

5.1.2.5   Change practice areas

Change is a fundamental organizational capability that enables the organization to adapt to its environment. Internal and external needs and a dynamic threat environment drive the Change capability. This capability affects digital solutions that meet the design requirements to create, protect, and deliver digital business value. It establishes the governance structure essential to coordinate digital business value solutions.

You may be familiar with the terms "release management" and "deployment management" in a technical context. However, from a systems perspective, it's essential to think of them in broader terms. Every change, whether strategic, tactical, administrative, or technical, requires coordination, environmental adaptation, moving something to a new environment (deployment), or making it available for use (release).

Practice areas:

- Change coordination
- Solution adaptation
- Release management
- Deployment management.

5.1.2.6   Execute practice areas

The Execute capability delivers created value that is appropriately protected. Its practice areas encompass providing access to digital products, services, and/or systems to authorized users; identifying, mitigating, and resolving system disruptions of the delivery of digital business value; and managing the overarching organizational infrastructure/platforms.

We use the term "productivity management" to be more reflective of intent regarding what other approaches call "incident management." It's not about managing the incident: it's about ensuring the restoration or maintenance of an acceptable level of productivity if and when a disruptive event occurs.

Practice areas:

- Provisioning
- Productivity management
- Problem management
- Infrastructure/platform management.

5.1.2.7   Innovate practice areas

The organization starts "where it is." That means everything the organization does is considered an innovation. Innovation is the introduction of something new.

Innovate, like Change, enables an organization to continually adapt to its environment in one of four ways: incremental, sustaining, adaptive, and disruptive (see the introduction to Chapter 2 and section 3.3.2 for specifics).

The Innovate capability measures the overall performance of organizational capabilities, activities, components, and systems that create, protect, and deliver digital business value. Its practice areas are catalog innovation opportunities, measure performance, and analyze performance gaps.

Practice areas:

- Continual innovation
- Performance measurement
- Gap analysis.

5.2   Application leverage in a complex adaptive system

"To improve the performance of a system, it's essential to understand the difference between complicated and complex systems. Managing complexity requires understanding the system and its subsystem exchanges and interactions, including the effectiveness and efficiency of the system as a whole."
Mind Tools Content Team (Mind Tools, 2024)

The CPD Model is a system escalation archetype (section 2.3.2) representing a CAS; it explains how the DVMS Z-X Model is put into action. Like any CAS, it must be influenced carefully to make it exhibit desirable behaviors.

Let's discuss the various behaviors of a CAS and how we can precisely identify and test each type with the help of the *Cynefin* framework. As we'll see in the next section, this framework enables leaders to understand challenges and make decisions. Once we identify the type and the desired extent of system behavioral change, we can choose and apply the most appropriate level of leverage.

5.2.1   Complicated is not complex

Determining whether a task is simple depends on whether the conditions and information needed for the task are readily available without requiring additional research or dependencies on third parties. A change is considered simple if it has a minimal impact on other components with no unintended consequences. The essential characteristic of a simple task is its predictability, with clear and direct links between cause and effect.

If a task requires further research to understand its complexity, it becomes more complicated and requires more steps. As the scope of effect expands to multiple system elements, the task becomes more complicated, but without necessarily being complex provided that the full impact is understood.

It becomes complex when a change or leverage point requires more work to understand potentially far-reaching implications for the rest of the system. Coping with complexity involves dealing with the interactions between system elements; it requires more steps, care, and diligence to achieve an outcome. The hallmark of complexity is the blurred lines between cause and effect combined with an unknown (or unknowable) set of interactions.

The most effective leaders understand that problem-solving is not a "one-size-fits-all" process. They know that their actions depend on the situation, and make better decisions by adapting their approach to changing circumstances.

Cynefin (Figure 5.1) is a useful decision-making framework that helps identify the type of problem the organization faces. David J. Snowden coined the term "Cynefin framework" in 1999 (Wikipedia, 2024a). He developed this framework by incorporating knowledge management and organizational strategy concepts. In collaboration with Mary Boone, he published the framework in the November 2007 issue of the *Harvard Business Review* (Snowden and Boone, 2007). The Cynefin framework is a problem-solving tool that categorizes situations into five domains based on cause-and-effect relationships. This categorization assists in accurately assessing the situation and responding appropriately.

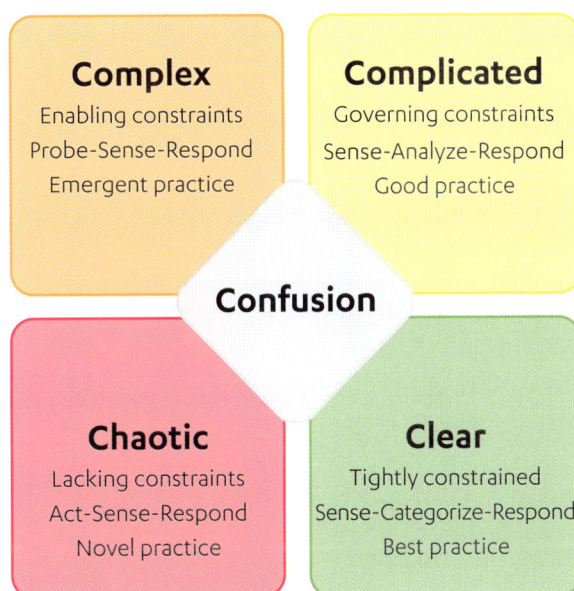

Figure 5.1 The Cynefin framework

The Cynefin framework applies in various scenarios to classify problems or decisions and take the appropriate action. It proves beneficial in product development, marketing, and organizational strategy. Additionally, it aids in making sound decisions during a crisis or emergency. When the framework is properly considered and applied, it can reduce the likelihood of using the same management style or decision-making approach in all situations. This, in turn, can save significant expenses for your team or organization. Instead, it encourages a flexible and adaptable decision-making process to adjust your management style based on your circumstances.

The five situational domains that the framework defines are:

- Clear
- Complicated
- Complex
- Chaotic
- Confusion.

Each of these domains has a specific decision-making approach that helps you make better sense of the situation and choose the most appropriate way forward.

5.2.2 Applying leverage

In his sequel to his popular TV series *Connections*, James Burke, a British science historian, introduced *The Day the Universe Changed* (Wikipedia, 2024f). The series revolved around the philosophical idea that the universe only exists as one perceives it through what one knows; therefore, when perception changes, this new insight means that the universe has changed (new perception means new reality). We are talking about this because changing the behavior of a complex system is easy; getting the desired behaviors and outcomes is exponentially more difficult.

As described in section 2.1.3, you cannot fix a complex adaptive system (CAS). Instead, you have to put in the work to coax it into changing behaviors (and potential structures) through a well-thought-out application of leverage. Getting the necessary buy-in to apply leverage may require organizational change management.

In her paper "Leverage points: Places to intervene in a system," Donella Meadows (1999) wrote:

> *"Folks who do systems analysis have a great belief in 'leverage points.' These are places within a complex system (a corporation, an economy, a living body, a city, an ecosystem) where a small shift in one thing can produce big changes in everything."*

We introduced the leverage points in section 2.1.3 grouped from low-order to high-order. Section 3.3 presented the list in numerical order from high-order impact to low. We reproduce the list below in the order Meadows used in her paper. As we said in Chapter 2, we strongly recommend reading the paper in its entirety.

- Low-order

  12   Constants, parameters, numbers – be aware of the risk of what gets measured gets done

  11   Stabilizing buffers (in systems speak, "stocks and flows")

  10   The structure of these stocks and flows

  9   System latency – specifically, the length of a delay relative to the rate of system change.

- Medium-order

  8   Negative feedback loop strength relative to the impact the organization tries to correct

  7   Gain driven by positive feedback loops

  6   Structure of information flows – i.e., who has access to specific information flows

  5   System rules – including constraints, rewards, and punishments.

- High-order

  4   Power to add, change, evolve, or self-organize system structure

  3   System goals (i.e., the goals of the system)

  2   Mindset or paradigm that leads to system goals, structure, rules, delays, and parameters

  1   Transcending paradigms – in other words, recognizing the belief that the current paradigm shouldn't (or can't) be changed.

As a thought exercise, what are the differences between:

- Low-order leverage points (9 to 12)
- Medium-order leverage points (5 to 8)
- High-order leverage points (1 to 4)?

The short answer is that low-order leverage points have the least impact on the system and potentially require the least thought to implement.

5.3   Creating a learning organization

A Vector Solutions blog post titled "What is a learning organization?" (Vector Solutions, 2019) references three influential thinkers in the learning organization thought domain.[40]

"Learning organizations are groups where individuals consistently enhance their ability to achieve their desired outcomes, cultivate new and expansive ways of thinking, unleash their collective aspirations, and develop their ability to see the bigger picture as a team. Learning organizations are groups in which individuals consistently enhance their ability to achieve their desired outcomes, cultivate new and expansiveways of thinking, unleash their collective aspirations, and develop their ability to see the bigger picture as a team."
Peter Senge (2006)

Senge's definition of a learning organization (above) includes places where people "expand their capacity to create," but also organizations "where new and expansive patterns of thinking are nurtured [and] ... collective aspiration is set free," and "where people are continually learning to see the whole together." So Senge's definition involves the learning by people, the conditions at the organization in which people learn, and a hint at learning that allows everyone at work to see a "whole together." That final point refers to systems thinking, which Senge argued is very important and will reoccur.

"The Learning Company is a vision of what might be possible. It is not brought about simply by training individuals; it can only happen as a result of learning at the whole organization level.

A Learning Company is an organization that facilitates the learning of all its members and continuously transforms itself."
Mike Pedler *et al.* (1996)

40   We've referenced Peter Senge (2006) extensively in this book. The Vector Solutions blog is a resource for more information, as are these two university sites: https://hbr.org/search?search_type=&term=learning+organization&term=&search_type=search-all and https://sloanreview.mit.edu/?s=Learning%20organization.

Pedler *et al.* use the term "learning company" instead of "learning organization," but are discussing the same thing. Notice that their definition points out that being a learning organization means more than just providing training. According to their explanation, a learning organization facilitates "the learning of all its members," learning occurs "at the whole organization level," and the learning of all organization members causes the organization to "continuously [transform] itself." Interestingly, their definition suggests all individuals learn, but the learning affects the entire organization and causes it to change continuously in response to that learning.

"Learning organizations are characterized by total employee involvement in a process of collaboratively conducted, collectively accountable change directed towards shared values or principles."
Watkins and Marsick (1992)

Watkins and Marsick's definition of a learning organization includes much of the same nomenclature for the involvement of employees in a collaborative effort that leads to change.

Let's look at the core takeaways:

- Expand the individual's capacity to create
- Nurture new and expansive patterns of thinking
- People are continually learning to see the whole together
- Learning occurs at the whole organization level (all individuals learn, but the learning affects the entire organization)
- Learning enables continual evolution (change) as a response to it
- Employees, in a collaborative effort, lead to change (shared values).

There is one more aspect of creating a learning organization that should be considered.

5.3.1 The learning organization and innovation

What are the characteristics of a learning organization? Senge (2006) suggests the following five characteristics:

- **Systems thinking** Organizations (and other human efforts) are systems. The "systems thinking" framework allows individuals to analyze businesses as entities within an ecosystem. A learning organization employs systems thinking to assess its enterprise in the context of interactions between its parts or functions in its environment. Instead of focusing on isolated parts or functions, this approach considers the organization as a whole. It helps to understand how the organization operates beyond its individual functional areas. By considering an organization as a CAS, it is possible to observe behaviors and optimize success in a chaotic environment by testing and selecting options to enhance performance. However, becoming a learning organization is not an automatic process but involves expanding existing characteristics and developing new ones to function effectively

- **Personal mastery** Personal mastery is the quality of being dedicated to acquiring and applying knowledge in practical ways to increase productivity, adaptability, and resilience. A workforce that learns more efficiently than its competitors has a significant advantage for the organization. Learning can occur in various ways and at different levels. Although on-the-job training is common, formal training is essential for individual growth and development. Personal mastery has a significant impact on individual and team performance, efficiency, and effectiveness, resulting in positive organizational outcomes

- **Mental models** Mental models are created by our brains as shortcuts to simplify complicated or complex things. They form the basis for assumptions and generalizations, and create a frame of reference that can impact what people can or cannot detect due to selective observation. As knowledge is acquired and actions are taken, mental models must be examined, tested, challenged, and modified

- **Shared vision** Creating a shared vision is key to uniting and motivating everyone in an organization. Leadership is critical in developing a vision that embodies the organizational goals, encouraging individuals to engage rather than simply follow directives. This shared vision guides actions and strategies, enhancing the organizational ability to create and deliver appropriately protected value. A unified vision motivates learning by promoting a shared identity and providing direction. Incorporating employees' visions is crucial, but traditional hierarchical structures can impede this process. Consequently, learning organizations often adopt flatter structures to foster collaboration and the creation of a shared vision

- **Team learning** Individual learning feeds into team learning, which hinges on collaboration and the sharing of ideas, making the team smarter than the sum of its members. This process not only accelerates staff education but also enhances organizational problem-solving capabilities through better access to knowledge. Learning organizations facilitate this dynamic by creating structures that promote team learning. In such environments, team knowledge – formed from the synthesis of individual expertise – boosts both the collective intelligence and each member's mastery. These organizations champion cross-team learning, significantly aided by the DVMS 3D Knowledge Model, which ensures transparency in work processes, communication, and innovation. This model is crucial for fostering an ecosystem where innovation thrives, propelled by the collective intelligence of the team.

Learning organizations don't just happen – there are specific reasons that prompt their development. As an organization grows, its learning ability might decrease due to rigid structures and thinking. The advantage of being a learning organization is that it provides a competitive edge by acquiring different strategies. Encouraging people to learn and innovate results in a more innovative environment. Problems will arise when the learning process stalls or loses ground. These issues can be identified and addressed, but some organizations struggle with embracing personal mastery as an intangible concept that is hard to quantify.

According to *The Dance of Change* (Senge *et al.*, 1999), some organizations struggle to become learning organizations due to a lack of time or commitment. In such cases, a mentor or coach knowledgeable about the concept of a learning organization may be necessary to guide the process. Organizations must become ambidextrous and capable of simultaneously working on and in a system to overcome these challenges (see section 5.4 for more details).

The CPD Model provides a systems archetype that helps us understand how CAS, such as businesses, adapt and change to meet their internal requirements, external needs, and a dynamic threat landscape. The DVMS Z-X Model's Innovate capability enables organizations to continually innovate and support how they adapt to their changing environment. The four aspects of innovation enable the organization to make objective decisions regarding the extent of change required to meet its needs. These four aspects cover everything from day-to-day changes to a shift in strategy, allowing for incremental, sustaining, adaptive, and disruptive changes (see sections 5.1.2.7 and 3.3.2).

5.3.2 The learning individual and innovation

In section 5.3.1, we discovered that personal mastery involves an individual's commitment to gaining knowledge. A workforce learning more efficiently than its competitors gives the organization a significant advantage. Learning isn't just about acquiring information: it's also about enhancing productivity by utilizing skills most effectively. The four aspects of Innovate help the organization make objective decisions about how much change is necessary to meet its needs.

So, how can we empower individuals to learn and use that knowledge to become more efficient and productive, and to help their organization become more competitive? It all starts with the organizational paradigm shift toward becoming a learning organization. Without this shift, individual mastery isn't possible, and it won't create the culture of individual mastery that aggregates to become the organizational "learning culture."

Systems thinking and using the 3D Knowledge Model provide a platform that supports individual learning and personal mastery. At the team level, this represents a shared vision of determining the extent of innovation. Think of it like three layers of bubble wrap, where the bottom bubble is the individual, the next is the team, and the top is the organization. Information, communication, and work flow horizontally and vertically in an interlocking matrix. This enables individuals and teams to quickly try out ideas, discarding ones that fail and innovating those that work. Decision-making takes place where the effect is felt.

This learning and innovation platform also provides transparency across the organization, with knowledge of what has happened, actions to be taken, and the potential resulting impact on future activity in the value chain. Full transparency enables the organization to quickly capitalize on innovative opportunities, solidify and improve core and mission-critical organizational capabilities, and cull outdated or inefficient activities. An organization can flatten its structure, streamline oversight and decision-making, and expedite adaptive and disruptive innovation to provide itself with nearly real-time capabilities to adapt to its environment.

5.4   Operate and innovate

Earlier, we talked about how organizations need to operate ("operating *on* the system") and innovate ("working *in* the system") simultaneously, and we described this as being "ambidextrous" (see sections 3.4.2 and 5.3.1).

"Operating on the system" means an organization works to create or improve its people, practices, and technology capabilities. Both the implementor's and auditor's perspectives are essential to this process, as they allow for planning, design, change, execution, and innovation to occur to create, protect, and deliver digital business value. It is possible to determine whether new or changed systems are fit for purpose and use by combining these perspectives.

Meanwhile, "working in the system" refers to what people in the organization do to achieve desired capabilities. This includes using data from the system to make informed decisions and identify potential innovation opportunities. Before an organization can innovate to improve outcomes, it must achieve stability. This can be compared to building a raft from the debris of a business when it's washed downstream and over rocks.

Once the organization has achieved a stable system state, the next step is to optimize the system and its capabilities to make them as efficient and effective as possible. An optimized system provides an operational baseline that works as well as possible. To reach this state, the organization must apply the right level of system leverage. Finally, once the system is stable and optimized, the organization can innovate and create new capabilities, or improve existing ones, to deliver digital business value.

5.4.1   Stabilize, optimize, and innovate

When you face a chaotic situation, it's essential to take control of what you can and manage what you cannot. Imagine yourself on a river with rapids – your priority is to keep yourself afloat and gather any floating debris to create a makeshift raft. This stabilizes the situation and ensures your survival. However, the rapids won't stop, so you have to make the best of what you have and prepare for what's to come. You look for materials to create a rudder, build a shelter on the deck, and store food. This is an innovation from a position of stability.

Now, you need to stabilize the situation by controlling what you can and managing the rest. Once you have a stable platform, you can optimize your capabilities and innovate to create, protect, and deliver digital business value. The DVMS FastTrack approach follows a phased approach based on the DVMS Z-X Model capabilities, which enable organizations to adapt to any situation quickly. This approach integrates control requirements with the underlying capabilities to deliver digital business value.

The DVMS FastTrack approach is used to adapt and implement new or changed capabilities of the underlying organizational DVMS. The initiation phase prepares the organization for the first stage, establishing a beachhead by ensuring basic controls are in place to stabilize and optimize organizational capabilities. Once the beachhead is secure, the foundation phase expands the defensible perimeter. The last phase establishes the capability to innovate continually.

Each organization must assess its internal needs, its external requirements, and a dynamic threat landscape in the context of its capabilities and digital assets. With the DVMS FastTrack approach, policies and resources are available to create, protect, and deliver digital business within the tolerances established by strategic policy. It may seem daunting, but with the right approach and tools, it is possible to innovate and thrive even in chaotic situations.

5.4.2   Being "ambidextrous"

As we stated above, an ambidextrous company works *on* and *in* a system simultaneously. This means the organization establishes a rhythm of innovation that fits its desired capabilities and budget, allowing it to create, protect, and deliver digital business value. To do this, the organization needs to take a systematic approach that identifies any performance gaps, determines the nature and severity of each gap, and agrees on the extent of innovation required to close or narrow the gap enough to meet its operating parameters.

An organization cannot achieve all of its objectives simultaneously, so it's important to establish a development rhythm that efficiently and effectively closes the organizational gap and creates, protects, and delivers digital business value. This way, the organization makes the most of its resources, improves its capabilities, and integrates those efforts into its operational rhythm. The goal is to learn how to apply the right leverage to achieve desired system behaviors and narrow the performance gap to meet the established policy parameters as a learning organization.

5.5   Bootstrapping a learning culture

Creating a learning organization depends on a strong learning culture – the learning organization and learning culture are two sides of the same coin. This culture represents the collective engagement of everyone within the organizational worldview and manifests itself in their behavior. While the leaders drive the culture from the top, it is how the individual engages with the paradigm that matters.

The DVMS CPD Model presents a visualization of an organization as a CAS. It helps organizations to adapt, survive, and thrive in chaotic environments by ensuring that the value created is protected and maintained at a level commensurate with its importance. By using a systems-thinking approach, the model aids organizations in self-organization and developing policies that safeguard digital business value while simultaneously creating it. It is a simple yet challenging concept that requires effort, but it is not rocket science.

Leaders must lead by example and embrace the new paradigm to create a learning culture that fosters collaboration and experimentation, removes blame, and learns. They must develop strategies, establish rules, and create policies that foster this idea. Furthermore, they should focus on continually improving and developing capabilities that align with this culture.

5.5.1　Start where you are

When attempting to change an organizational culture, the first step is to analyze, document and understand the impact of the current culture, including positive and negative behaviors.

The next step is to consider and define the desired culture and then understand the magnitude of the change required and the effort needed to achieve it. It is essential to recognize that changing culture is a long-term undertaking and will not happen overnight. Rather than focusing on the daunting task of changing the entire culture, it is more beneficial to identify the gap between the current state and the desired state and incrementally work toward closing that gap.

To achieve lasting change, the organization must create a capability for continually monitoring its culture and identifying areas that require attention. The DVMS CPD Model facilitates this approach by supporting the selection of positive cultural behaviors.

It is essential to recognize that changing culture requires total buy-in from the entire organization and starts at the top, with senior leadership leading by example. This will create a new way of engaging with the organizational paradigm that individuals will follow. Although changing culture can be difficult and time-consuming, it is possible with the right approach and commitment.

5.5.2　Curate culture

*"**Curate** – verb: 2. To select and bring together (people or groups) for a purpose that is dependent on the specific skills or talents of the members."*
The Merriam-Webster Dictionary

Perhaps we could add "behaviors" to that list to make it relevant to our discussion.

Numerous articles and papers offer diverse perspectives and methods for modifying people's behavior. Jeremy Nicholson, writing a blog post for *Psychology Today* (Nicholson, 2021), provides the most effective approach to behaviors, which involves selective reinforcement with positive outcomes. This entails rewarding the behaviors that you want them to repeat, while not rewarding, and redirecting them away from, the behaviors that you want them to stop.

There follows Nicholson's proposed methods of changing people's behavior.

Changing the behavior of others for the better (Nicholson, 2021)

- **Learn what is reinforcing to the individual** Affectionate regard, positive attention, and kind words and help can all be reinforcing at particular times. Furthermore, each person may have their unique preferences. One person might prefer a compliment, while another might prefer help with a problem. To truly become influential, learn what someone specifically finds rewarding. Then, use it to better shape their behaviors and your relationship with them

- **Identify positive and negative behaviors** All behaviors are not equal. Some are better than others for an individual's well-being, their performance, or the continuation of your relationship with them. Thus, it is important to tell the difference, especially noting the behaviors that are positive and constructive. After all, those will be the ones you will need to reward in the future (while learning to ignore and redirect the rest)

- **Reward positive behaviors immediately** For consequences to be most effective, they should occur right after the behavior. When you identify the other person performing a positive behavior, be sure to reward it in the moment (especially with an expression of regard and support). Even small positive behaviors should be reinforced with attention and a smile. If the situation warrants, follow up with further positive reinforcement

- **Ignore and redirect negative behaviors** Many people make the mistake of paying attention to someone who is acting in a hurtful, grumpy, or obstinate way. Unfortunately, that attention reinforces those bad behaviors and makes them continue. Furthermore, although it might feel tempting in the moment, a reliance on punishment only leads to bad relationships. Therefore, it is best to use extinction and differential reinforcement of alternative behaviors. Put simply, do not give them attention for the negative behavior (extinction); refocus them on doing something positive (alternative behavior), and then reward them for that alternative behavior (differential reinforcement). That approach improves the relationship with whoever you are redirecting and rewarding too.

Chris Edmonds explains, in his book *The Culture Engine* (Edmonds, 2014), the importance of a "cultural constitution" for organizations to reach their full potential. He believes that the culture should accurately represent organizational values and that leaders should lead by example. By doing so, Edmonds argues that a values-aligned culture can be established based on an organizational constitution.

A cultural constitution sets clear expectations for individual behavior within the organizational worldview. It communicates, models, and enforces expected behavior. However, creating and living by a cultural constitution is not easy, and requires hard work and dedication for long-term, lasting results.

The DVMS CPD Model helps integrate the critical aspects of a cultural constitution. At the same time, the DVMS 3D Knowledge Model enables the transparency and communication necessary for curating value-aligned cultural behaviors within the organization.

5.6   Chapter takeaways

Shaping outcomes requires context and expectations. For the DVMS, treated as an overlay, everything the organization already does maps to one or more of the MVC. Each capability aggregates practice areas enumerated in Appendix A.

Another aspect of the ability to shape outcomes is appropriate decision-making, which is why we included the Cynefin framework, introduced in section 5.2. Cynefin is useful to facilitate decisions about the application of leverage (both selecting leverage points and where and how to apply them).

As noted in section 3.2.4, we view the learning organization in the context of a learning system. In this chapter, we connected the idea of a learning organization to one that works both *on* and *in* the system – what we described as "ambidextrous."

Finally, we connected the idea of a learning organization to one that exhibits a learning culture. Leaders, and a learning organization, understand and accept the responsibility to curate the culture by accepting the responsibility and accountability to demonstrate the expected behaviors, in and outside of the work environment.

CHAPTER 6
Building the team

6 Building the team

Let's create a team that spearheads the adoption of a new paradigm and modifies it to suit the internal organizational requirements, external demands, and the constantly changing threat landscape. This approach requires us to develop new capabilities while improving existing ones, creating a highly adaptive and resilient organization that continually innovates. Our goal is to deliver digital business value to stakeholders while protecting them.

6.1 Praxis and the DVMS

This section introduces the Digital Value Management System *Praxis*, a framework for implementing the DVMS theory. It describes how mental models enable and shape new ways of thinking that result in a systems approach to achieving desired outcomes. The section also explores the capabilities and practice areas of the DVMS Z-X Model and touches on the role of culture in making it all happen.

The Praxis website[41] provides free access to this scalable portfolio, program, and project management framework. It includes a body of knowledge, methodology, competency framework, and capability maturity model, supported by a knowledge base of resources and an encyclopedia. Praxis is entirely free to use, and you can tailor it to fit your needs, provided you acknowledge its source and make your work available to others free of royalties.

Section 6.3 covers this idea in more detail.

6.1.1 Praxis – theory to practice

We use the term "Praxis" in the context of transforming theory into practice. This involves engaging, applying, exercising, realizing, and practicing an idea or theory.

- **Engaging** involves understanding and exploring an idea or theory to implement it
- **Applying** requires finding the most suitable methods to solve problems and achieve positive results
- **Exercising** involves testing and working within the system to apply the idea or theory
- **Realizing** involves identifying and addressing gaps between the idea or theory and its practical application
- **Practicing** refers to using the applied idea or theory in real-life situations.

6.1.2 Praxis and the DVMS Model

In applying Praxis, we utilize four knowledge domains to turn the ideas behind the DVMS into the practice of digital value management (Figure 6.1).

- **Knowledge of the discipline** Digital value management represents the contextual and managerial capabilities an adopting organization needs in order to successfully create, protect, and deliver digital business value. This domain includes knowledge of the CPD Model, ERM (DBR – digital business risk), DVMS as an overlay, and the minimum viable capabilities of the DVMS Z-X Model

---

41   https://www.praxisframework.org/

- **Approach using capabilities, practice areas, and practices** This knowledge domain covers the practices and outcomes necessary to create, protect, and deliver digital business value. Digital value management uses the "stabilize, optimize, and innovate" approach of the DVMS FastTrack approach. This includes the 3D Knowledge Model, the DVMS Z-X Model capabilities, and continual innovation

- **Competence – knowledge, skills, and experience** This domain covers the knowledge, skills, experience, and culture necessary to create, protect, and deliver digital business value. The adopting organization must demonstrate competency in three areas:

  · Oversight, leadership, and sponsorship

  · Portfolio, program, and project management

  · Architecture, implementation, and audit

- **Maturity – organizational attributes of effectiveness** This knowledge domain covers the organizational capabilities and maturity of practices. It includes the Digital Value Capability Maturity Model (DVCMM) assessment of Govern, Assure, Plan, Design, Change, Execute, and Innovate organizational capabilities.

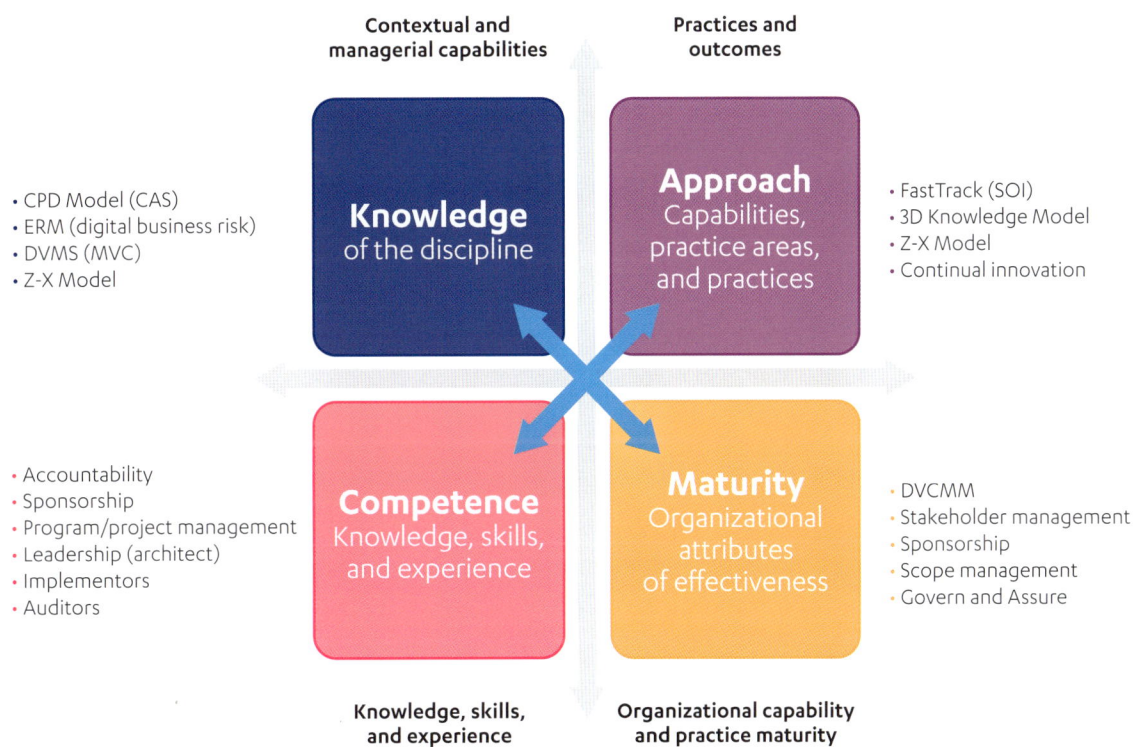

Figure 6.1 The Praxis of the DVMS

6.1.3   DVMS Z-X Model practice areas

For a detailed description of the numbered practice areas (e.g., GO-1, AS-1), see Appendix A.

6.1.3.1 Govern

The Govern capability practice areas (Figure 6.2) include identifying critical business systems and determining the digital business risk posture based on the potential impact of system compromise. The CPD Model is a crucial component of the DVMS that operationalizes the Z-X Model capabilities; it provides objective and subjective performance gap evaluations.

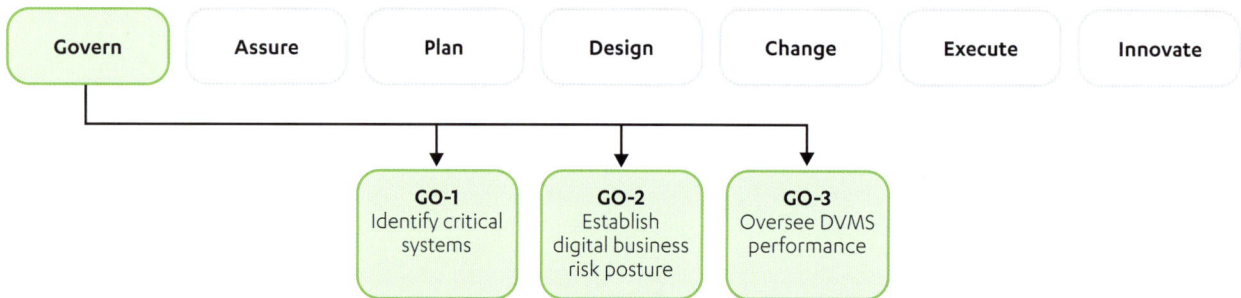

Figure 6.2 Govern practice areas

6.1.3.2 Assure

The practice areas associated with the Assure capability (Figure 6.3) support the determination that the organization is effectively implementing its strategic policies and that its capabilities are efficient and effective. This capability includes four practice areas: establishing assurance criteria, assessing the performance of strategic policies, evaluating operational capabilities, and ensuring the accuracy of performance measurement.

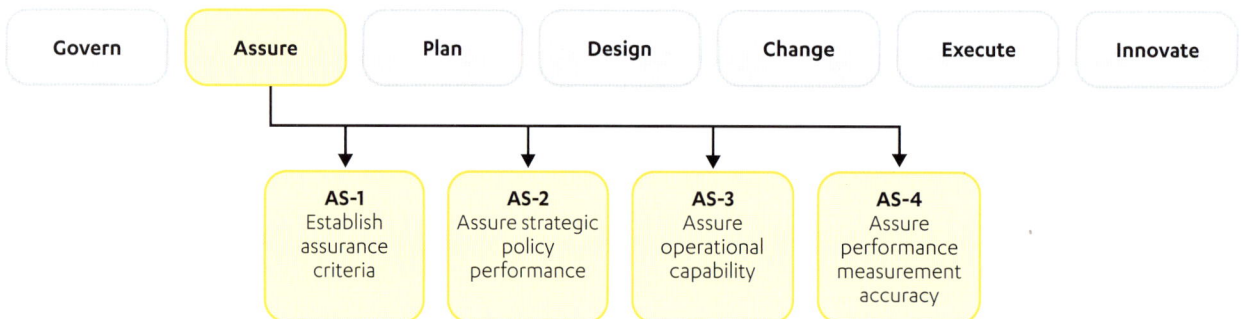

Figure 6.3 Assure practice areas

6.1.3.3 Plan

Planning (Figure 6.4) is a vital aspect of achieving success in an organization. As noted in section 3.5.2, these capabilities are interrelated. The most obvious aspect of this interdependence is the relationship between Plan and the Govern and Assure capabilities (note the first two practice areas in Figure 6.4). Specifically, the Plan capability "plans" (or bootstraps) two other capabilities. Strategy-risk management puts the organizational risk appetite into action, while portfolio, program, and project management oversees the development of new or improved organizational capabilities. Knowledge management is crucial for creating and maintaining organizational knowledge in a learning organization.

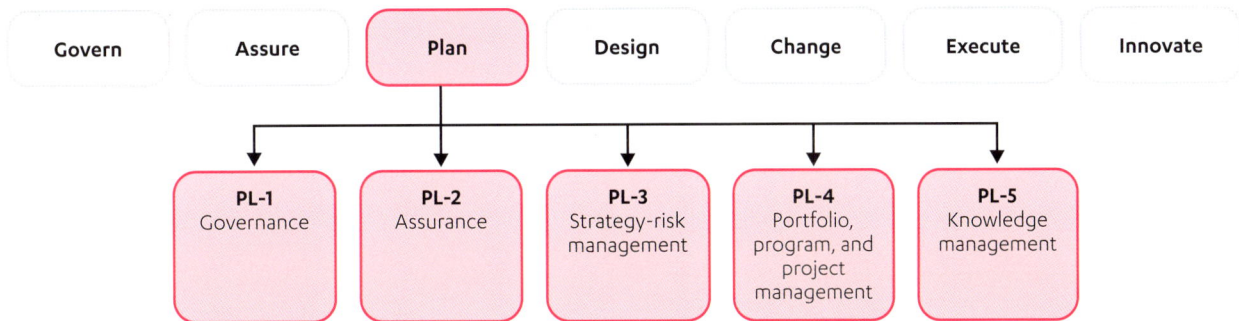

Figure 6.4 Plan practice areas

6.1.3.4 Design

The Design capability has two practice areas (Figure 6.5) that ensure the accurate representation and implementation of appropriate system design approaches. These areas are crucial in creating, protecting, and delivering digital business value to stakeholders, resulting in improved organizational capabilities. The system architecture practice area provides the basis for creating, protecting, and delivering digital business value. The configuration management practice area is crucial to successful system architecture and the resulting management of digital business value.

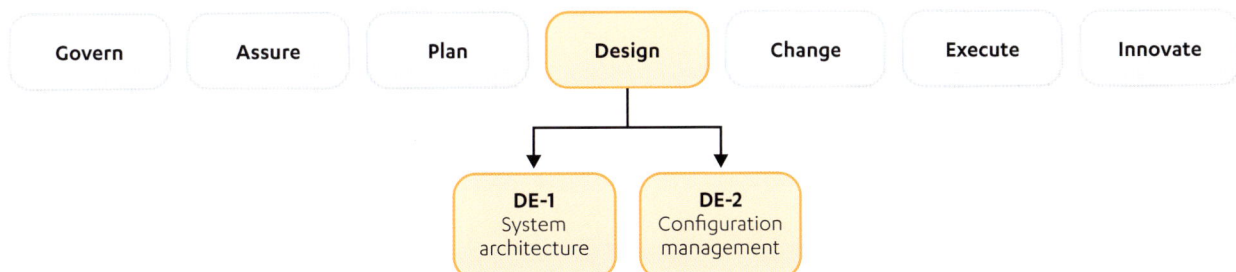

Figure 6.5 Design practice areas

6.1.3.5   Change

The CPD Model operationalization of the DVMS Z-X Model is crucial to the DVMS as an overlay. The Change practice areas (Figure 6.6) are essential organizational capabilities that enable adaptability, resilience, and continual innovation. They include coordinating change, adapting solutions to the organizational context, releasing new or modified capabilities, and managing their deployment. This is vital for working both *on* and *in* a system.

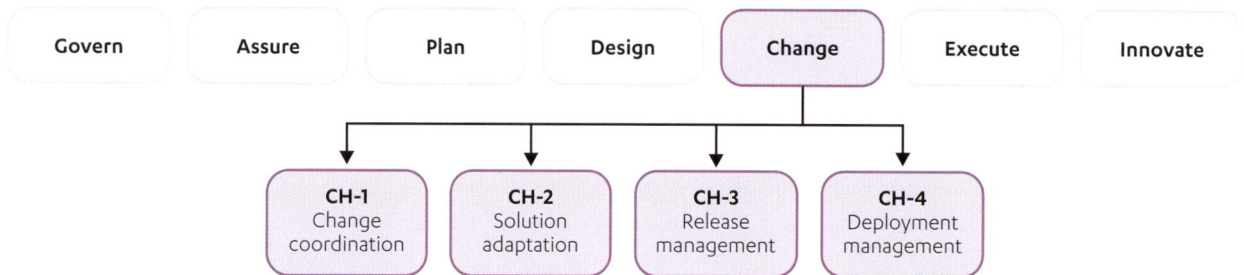

Govern	Assure	Plan	Design	**Change**	Execute	Innovate

CH-1 Change coordination	CH-2 Solution adaptation	CH-3 Release management	CH-4 Deployment management

Figure 6.6 Change practice areas

6.1.3.6   Execute

The Execute capability practice areas (Figure 6.7) are responsible for delivering digital business value to stakeholders and working *in* the system. The "provisioning" practice area provides stakeholders with access to the business system to create digital business value. In the event of system outages or performance gaps, the incident and problem management practice areas mitigate the issues by identifying and removing systemic problems. This requires managing the infrastructure and delivery platforms of the business system.

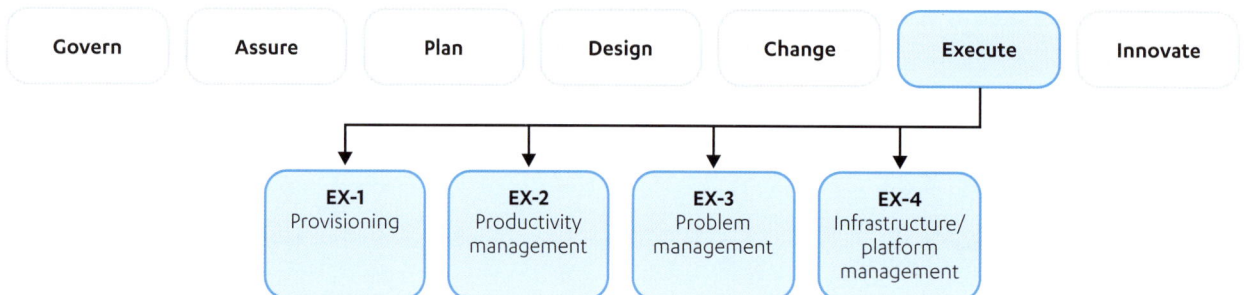

Govern	Assure	Plan	Design	Change	**Execute**	Innovate

EX-1 Provisioning	EX-2 Productivity management	EX-3 Problem management	EX-4 Infrastructure/ platform management

Figure 6.7 Execute practice areas

6.1.3.7 Innovate

The Innovate capability (Figure 6.8) of the DVMS Z-X Model is crucial to the success of modern digital business systems. Leveraging the CPD Model, designed as a CAS archetype, enables identification and measurement of performance gaps. It also facilitates selecting the appropriate level of innovation required to improve performance. There are four different types of innovation – incremental, sustaining, adaptive, and disruptive – supported by the DVMS. This system is scalable, and organizations of any size can be use it to maintain continual innovation.

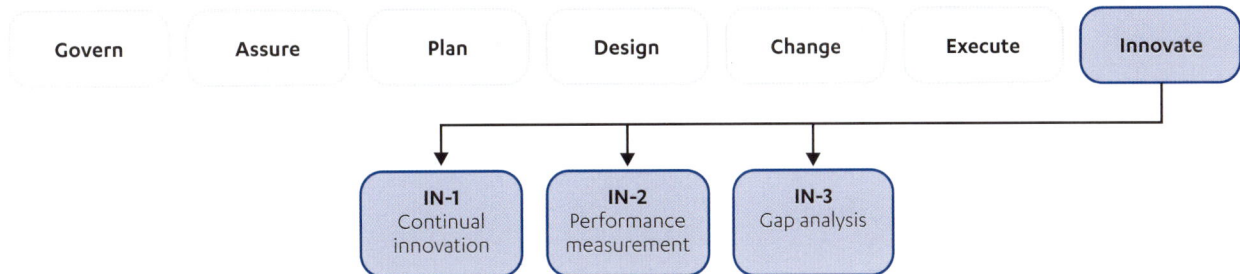

Figure 6.8 Innovate practice areas

6.2 The risk team

We introduced the risk team concept in section 4.3; we cover it here in more detail. Figure 6.9 presents a high-level overview focusing on just the team. The concept of having a risk team is not novel, and several articles and papers provide detailed descriptions of what constitutes a risk team. However, one article the author read listed 22 roles, which is not practical for most organizations that aim to create, protect, and deliver digital business value, irrespective of their size. Therefore, this section proposes a lean approach for achieving the same objectives.

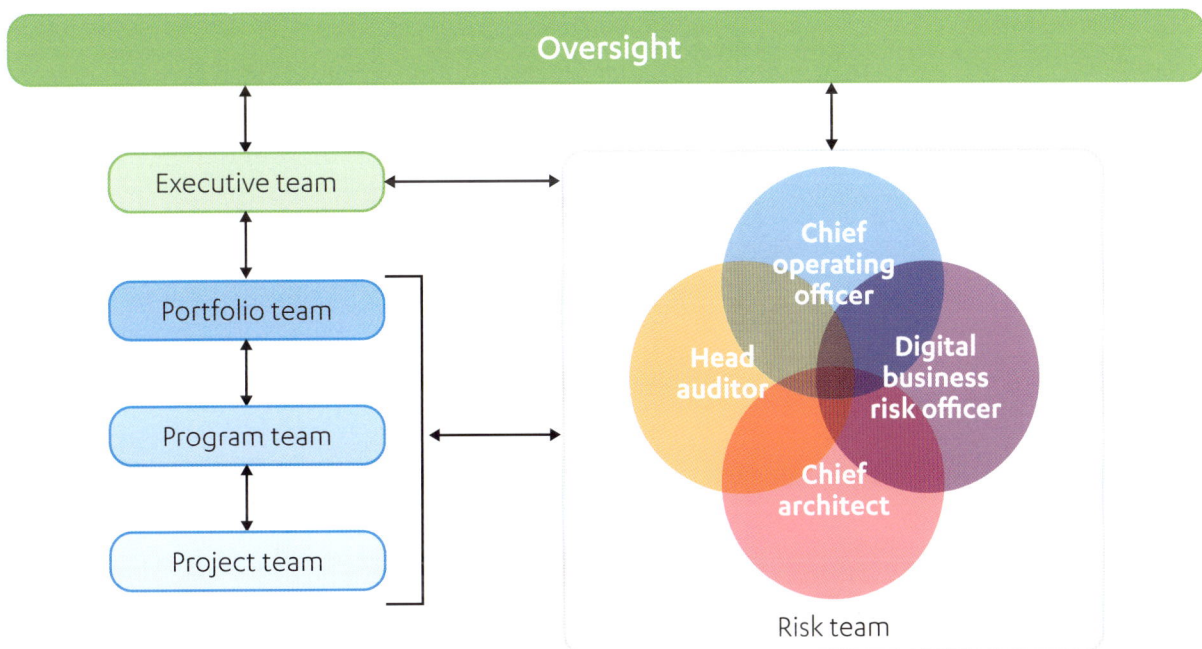

Figure 6.9 The risk team

The DVMS is an overlay that easily scales to fit organizations of all sizes. It is not a one-size-fits-all solution; however, as an overlay, it can be adjusted to suit the unique needs of any organization. This section introduces our concept of a risk team in an organization that adopts the DVMS as an overlay. The roles we cover are not job descriptions, but roles that someone in the organization fulfills. Even in the smallest of organizations, these roles are fulfilled by someone. In a larger organization, they may be performed by one person or more in a team or a department. The crucial aspects to remember are the outcomes and the relationships.

The risk team offers advice to those who manage the organization, including the executive management team and the portfolio, program, and project managers. By working collaboratively, the team provides a comprehensive view of enterprise risk to various stakeholders. This strategy is different from the trend of appointing a tech or cybersecurity expert to the board for oversight. The risk team is better suited to provide advice and enable the board to focus on its oversight role. This integrated approach eliminates information silos and ensures a holistic approach to creating, protecting, and delivering digital business value.

6.2.1   Chief operating officer

In any organization, there is a person who takes on the role of overseeing operations. In smaller organizations, this person is often called the "boss," while larger and more complex organizations typically have a dedicated manager or director of operations. The COO fulfills this role in a large organization. Regardless of the specific job title, the head of operations is responsible for leading the risk team, ensuring it provides accurate advice to the board and executive team, and assisting management in creating rules and policies to execute the organizational strategic objectives, ensure performance, and deliver digital business value to stakeholders. They work closely with the portfolio, program, and project management teams to provide guidance and support for creating or improving capabilities that align with the organizational strategic objectives.

6.2.2   Digital business risk officer

The role of the DBRO (aka "head of digital business risk") is a construct of the DVMS. Given the current business climate, it's inconceivable that any business, short of a lemonade stand, can operate without the systems that create organizational value. That is why we created strategy-risk as a construct in the CPD Model to emphasize the integration of strategy and ERM as the drivers of creating rules and policies used by management to create or improve existing organizational capabilities.

As with the chief operating officer, the DBRO is a role that may be shared as the organization grows and becomes more complex. However, the DBRO's role is to ensure that the risk team takes a holistic view of the risk to organizational digital business value in the overall context of ERM.

The DBRO is crucial to formulating rules and policies that lead to the organizational capability to create digital business value, protect it at a level commensurate with its importance, and deliver it to the stakeholders.

6.2.3   Chief architect

The role of the chief architect is not technical; rather, this role is critical as an advocate for stakeholder interests. It requires the chief architect to work closely with other risk management team members and offer timely and accurate guidance to those overseeing the organizational operations. To succeed in this role, the chief architect must deeply understand how the organization works as a CAS. This includes comprehending any proposed innovation-related risks and benefits, and effectively communicating them to stakeholders and decision-makers.

In addition, the chief architect collaborates with the portfolio, program, and project management teams to implement strategic policies effectively.

6.2.4   Head auditor

The DVMS is used as an overlay to surface performance gaps that impede the organizational capability to create, protect, and deliver digital business value. The CPD Model, as an archetype of a CAS, requires a risk-based approach to assurance. Risk-based assurance fundamentally requires that auditors understand the system under audit and express confidence that the artifacts produced by the system accurately represent its performance. Therefore, the CPD Model integrates the implementor and auditor teams in identifying measures and metrics that satisfy both teams' needs.

With an intimate understanding of the system, the head auditor can accurately assess the artifacts produced by the system, express an assessment of its performance, and confidently report on its performance. They work with the risk team and help formulate the rules and policies that create new capabilities or improve existing ones.

The head auditor advises those who provide oversight, the executive team, and the portfolio, program, and project teams regarding the capability to assess the execution of its strategic policies accurately.

6.3   The Praxis framework and the risk team

As noted in section 6.1, a scalable portfolio, program, and project management framework called "Praxis" is free to access on the internet. The DVMS Institute suggests using an appropriate adaptation of the Praxis framework to suit your organizational need. Additionally, accredited training and exams are offered through APMG International.

6.3.1   Why recommend a portfolio, program, and project framework?

An organization adopting the DVMS as an overlay can create or enhance new capabilities. Depending on the size and complexity of the organization, it may require a system to manage resources automatically.

The Praxis framework is structured to handle projects, programs, and portfolios in a nested manner. As the organization evolves in size and complexity, the framework scales with it. Those familiar with agile will appreciate the inclusion of agile-like methods.

The Praxis framework is highly scalable and complete in its capabilities, yet not overly complex. It supports small and large organizations, even those without a project (or program) management office (PMO).

6.3.2   CPD portfolio of programs

Portfolio management is usually taken care of by large organizations, which may even be global in their scope. This is overseen by a high-ranking executive and is subject to board review. Transparency is key in portfolio management, since significant organizational resources are invested in the underlying programs and projects. If an organization successfully adopts the DVMS Z-X Model (minimum viable capabilities) and efficiently generates and effectively delivers digital business value to its stakeholders, it constantly innovates, making it highly flexible and resilient in its environment.

6.3.3   CPD program of projects

Related projects are often grouped together into programs. These programs may require a higher sponsorship level, especially if they impact multiple business units. This sponsorship usually comes from the management level to which the stakeholders report. When interacting with the risk team, the process is similar to that for individual projects. However, the level of interaction is at the business unit level, which normally carries a higher level of risk and requires executive sponsorship. The executive sponsor's role is not just symbolic, as they have a personal stake in program success and are ultimately accountable for its outcome.

6.3.4   CPD project

We should talk about the project and its connection with the risk team. For a project to be carried out effectively, approval is needed to use resources and reach a specific goal. Generally, an executive sponsor is assigned with the project approval. The risk team guides the sponsor and project management regarding the project and its relation to other projects (3D Knowledge Model). As organizational size and project complexity increase, they may group similar projects into programs for better management.

6.4   Chapter takeaways

As with previous chapters, everything is connected to everything else. We introduced Praxis as a way to turn theory into practice – and as a framework to manage the gamut of portfolios, programs, and projects.

We presented a brief overview of the practice areas associated with each of the MVC. You'll find more details in Appendix A.

This chapter also revisited the risk team in the context of the Praxis framework.

CHAPTER 7
Decisions and outcomes

7 Decisions and outcomes

In his book *The Fifth Discipline*, Peter Senge (2006) discusses systems thinking and its role in enabling an organization to become a "learning organization." The key to the learning organization is the willingness of the individual to pursue learning to achieve personal mastery. The organization actively encourages individuals to learn and innovate to help the organization adapt to its chaotic environment. Personal mastery is at the core of a learning organization, expressed by team contributions, resulting in team mastery, which is how the organization realizes the benefits of individual achievements.

In this chapter we look at the outcomes sought by the organization, and how a learning organization, in the context of an organizational capability to innovate, synthesizes a learning cascade. We'll also explore using a decision tool to help the organization properly identify the problem or gap in performance and select the appropriate leverage points to coax the value management system to close or narrow that gap.

7.1 Becoming a learning organization

We introduced Senge's five disciplines of the learning organization in section 5.3.1. Here we list them as a refresher:

- Systems thinking
- Personal mastery
- Mental models
- Shared vision
- Team learning.

While these disciplines will likely develop separately within an organization, the combination is critical to success. Systems thinking provides a different way of seeing the organization in its ecosystem, establishing a holistic approach to managing complexity by supporting both the revision of existing mental models and the creation of new ones. Personal mastery forms the basis of team learning, making the combined group intelligence greater than that of any individual member. All of this must occur within the context of a shared organizational vision.

7.1.1 A learning organization

In *The Fifth Discipline*, Senge (2006) discusses the concepts behind a learning organization, what it is, and why it's essential to become one. Learning organizations just don't pop into existence. Becoming a learning organization results from systems thinking and looking at the whole organization.

7.1.1.1 Metanoia

"Metanoia" is a term for a significant transformation or change of heart. Senge uses the term to mean "a shift of mind" in the context of the "Aha" moments that result from learning and discovery. When applied to a learning organization, metanoia involves recognizing the need to approach digital value differently – impacting the whole organization. In this case, the metanoia is the change from "creating *then* protecting" to "creating *and* protecting," and how that changes the approach to achieving organizational goals – it's about a change in thinking about organizational risk.

7.1.1.2   Self-limiting or sustaining growth

Systems thinking is a comprehensive approach to solving problems that emphasizes how different parts of a system are interconnected. It is especially helpful in analyzing self-limiting and self-sustaining behaviors.

The term "self-limiting behaviors" refers to the ability of the system to regulate its growth and maintain balance with its environment. This concept is often used in the context of population growth, where factors like resource availability, predation, and disease limit a population's size. Self-limiting behaviors work as a form of negative feedback, allowing the system to respond to changes in its environment by adjusting its growth rate. For example, when the US National Park Service allowed the elimination of wolves, an alpha predator, from Yellowstone National Park, it resulted in unexpected changes to the overall biodiversity in the park, including even changing the course of a river.

On the other hand, "self-sustaining behaviors" refers to maintaining system structure and function over time. This concept is often used in ecological systems, where a healthy ecosystem can maintain its biodiversity and productivity over time. Self-sustaining behaviors work as a form of positive feedback, allowing the system to reinforce its structure and function. As in the example above, the reintroduction of wolves to the park achieved a self-sustaining ecosystem.

In systems thinking, self-limiting and self-sustaining behaviors can be compared and contrasted based on their feedback mechanisms. Self-limiting behaviors work with negative feedback, which helps to regulate growth and maintain balance within a system. In contrast, self-sustaining behaviors work with positive feedback, which helps reinforce a system's structure and function. Both types of feedback are essential for maintaining a healthy system, but they operate differently and can affect the system's overall behavior.

7.1.1.3   Identify patterns that control events

To manage digital value effectively, one must understand the patterns that control events to make better decisions. This requires thinking differently, choosing the appropriate leverage, and determining where and how to apply it. To understand problems, determine their extent, and formulate how to probe and respond, we recommend Cynefin as a decision-making tool. Combining Cynefin with the Innovate capability and DVMS CPD Model enables an organization to make better decisions, select the appropriate response, and apply the appropriate leverage. A CAS comprises numerous components and behaviors, making it challenging. Therefore, using models and patterns can help the organization make the right decisions to deliver digital business value to stakeholders.

7.1.2   A learning organization and the DVMS

To become a learning organization requires an organizational "change of perspective."

"One's destination is never a place, but a new way of seeing things."
Henry Miller

Thinking closely about Henry Miller's quote, the organizational journey starts with a change of perspective, and that perspective continually evolves as the organization learns more and develops its organizational capabilities. This results in the continual growth of learning, and the increased adaptability and resilience of the organization.

Let's examine how a learning organization relates to the DVMS, using Senge's five disciplines as a basis.

7.1.2.1 Systems thinking

The concept of a learning organization is rooted in systems thinking, focusing on the business as a whole and its environment rather than its parts. The DVMS CPD Model embodies systems-thinking principles, depicting the organization as a CAS. This is operationalized through the DVMS Z-X Model, which details steps for the organization to protect digital business value and achieve its desired paradigm.

7.1.2.2 Personal mastery

Becoming a successful learning organization requires individuals to master relevant skills. Learning means applying knowledge to boost productivity, flexibility, and resilience. The DVMS 3D Knowledge Model aids in merging individual and team learning, enhancing group development. Together, individuals and teams can find innovations and use the model to track work flow, communication, and ideas.

7.1.2.3 Mental models

As humans, we often use mental shortcuts to understand complex topics better. One such model is the DVMS CPD Model, which describes organizational behavior as a CAS within a business environment. The addition of the DVMS Z-X Model enables organizations to identify the necessary improvements required to create, protect, and deliver digital business value. Additionally, the DVMS 3D Knowledge Model emphasizes the importance of transparency in organizational work, communication, and innovation, essential for achieving personal and team mastery.

7.1.2.4 Shared vision

Having a shared vision is crucial to foster a sense of unity and motivation among employees in an organization. This is where leadership plays a key role by curating the desired culture. The DVMS is based on the belief that organizations must provide adequately protected digital business value to their stakeholders. The DVMS Z-X Model outlines the fundamental capabilities an organization must possess to achieve this objective, while the DVMS 3D Knowledge Model ensures transparency in workflow, communication, and innovation. Lastly, the CPD Model facilitates the sharing of organizational capabilities, components, behaviors, and understanding, and operationalizes the DVMS Z-X Model to achieve the organizational paradigm.

7.1.2.5 Team learning

A team's knowledge comes together in the form of team learning, where each member achieves a degree of mastery and shares it with the team. The team's collaborative learning process enhances the team itself and its members, increasing their command of a subject. A learning organization fosters an environment that facilitates cross-team learning. This is primarily enabled through the DVMS 3D Knowledge Model, which represents the transparency of work, communication, and innovation that is fundamental to the functioning of a learning organization. The organization gains visibility as work and communication flow, leading to the realization of innovative ideas.

7.2 Enabling the learning cascade

The DVMS, its mental models, and approaches to systems thinking and enabling the learning organization result in a synthesis that creates the conditions we refer to as a "learning cascade."

---

*"**Cascade** – noun: 2a. Something arranged or occurring in a series or in a succession of stages so that each stage derives from or acts upon the product of the preceding."*
The Merriam-Webster Dictionary

This section explores how the DVMS models, systems thinking, and the learning organization create an environment that fosters individual and team learning. This leads to a highly adaptive, resilient organization that continually learns and improves. To achieve this, it is essential to avoid repeating past mistakes and approach problems with fresh perspectives.

Remember Senge's Law 1: "Today's problems come from yesterday's solutions." So, it's necessary to embrace new ways of thinking and approach challenges with a different mindset for new and effective solutions; think differently.

7.2.1 The learning cascade

The individual's commitment to learning is the genesis of a learning organization. It starts and ends with the individual. However, the organization must create the conditions necessary for the individual to learn and grow. So, let's think of this as a top-down, bottom-up reinforcing system archetype. The more individuals are encouraged and supported to learn and achieve personal mastery, the more learning occurs; the more team learning happens, the more benefits accrue to the organization that reaps the benefits and, in turn, provides more opportunities and incentives, and so on.

Three models enable this synthesis and subsequent learning cascade:

- The DVMS CPD Model
- The DVMS Z-X Model (Innovate capability)
- The DVMS 3D Learning Model.

7.2.1.1 The DVMS CPD Model

To become a learning organization, the organization must decide to change its worldview or paradigm to support the concepts of systems thinking and the aspects of a learning organization. That doesn't happen with the wave of a wand: it starts with the leadership painting a picture of a learning organization so that each individual in the organization can see themselves in that picture – learning, growing, and contributing to their team and the organizational achievements. Leadership must provide the necessary degrees of freedom for the individual to learn, fail, and try again. Experience is what we get when things don't go as expected. So, failure is part of learning.

The change to the paradigm is reflected in its rules and objectives, which result in policies and establishing the tolerances that management uses to create or enhance organizational capabilities. This makes the organizational commitment to individual learning part of the fabric of the organizational operations and culture.

7.2.1.2   The DVMS Z-X Model

The Innovate capability has four aspects that help to drive learning by using Cynefin to make decisions about the extent of innovation required. Each innovation helps the organization to gain more knowledge about working on the DVMS. As the organization becomes more familiar with the problem (performance gaps), it learns more about the solutions (the four aspects of innovation), and this cycle continues. The amount of learning gained depends on the problem's complexity and the innovation's extent.

7.2.1.3   The DVMS 3D Knowledge Model

If the four Innovate aspects are the fuel, then the 3D Knowledge Model acts as the match. Learning occurs when individuals thoroughly understand how work, communication, and innovation flow, as the 3D Knowledge Model explains. The model's structure ensures that all value actors, regardless of their organizational level (strategic, management, or operations), have complete knowledge and transparency of all innovation activities. This approach eliminates knowledge and functional silos that hinder organizational learning. It's not akin to the Borg Collective or a hive mentality, but rather a closely linked network of individuals and teams with in-depth knowledge and comprehension of their work's impact on others and vice versa.

7.2.2   The 3D Knowledge Model and the freedom to innovate

The 3D Knowledge Model is a critical tool for understanding how communication, work, and innovation function in a complex system. As a software developer working on a team that is creating a mobile application to help a sales engineer capture specifications for a custom power supply for a new product for a customer, you play a vital role in this model. It is crucial to comprehend how communication, work, and innovation operate within the 3D Knowledge Model in this context.

Communication happens in all three axes of the 3D Knowledge Model. In the above example, the Z-axis enables you to capture the customer's technical specifications on-site and provide them with design, unit pricing, and shipping lead time. As a programmer, you create software that formats the sales engineer's specifications as input to the legacy design configurator. You understand the value of this software for the entire product development lifecycle. Additionally, you provide proper documentation for your code to ensure a smooth handoff to the next steps and facilitate seamless communication.

As work moves through the value stream, different individuals contribute to its overall value by performing various actions. In some cases, your team might incorporate another team's work into your own, or another team might repurpose or reuse something your team created. The 3D Knowledge Model is designed to break down silos and promote collaboration, as each team refers to different parts of the model to ensure that its work aligns with the organizational strategic and operational goals.

Innovation is present in every aspect of the 3D Knowledge Model (as shown in Figure 7.1) and ranges from small, incremental changes to larger, disruptive ones. Examples of such innovations include developing standard capabilities to maintain competitiveness, changing policies to reduce cycle times significantly, and replacing outdated systems to enter new markets and free up resources.

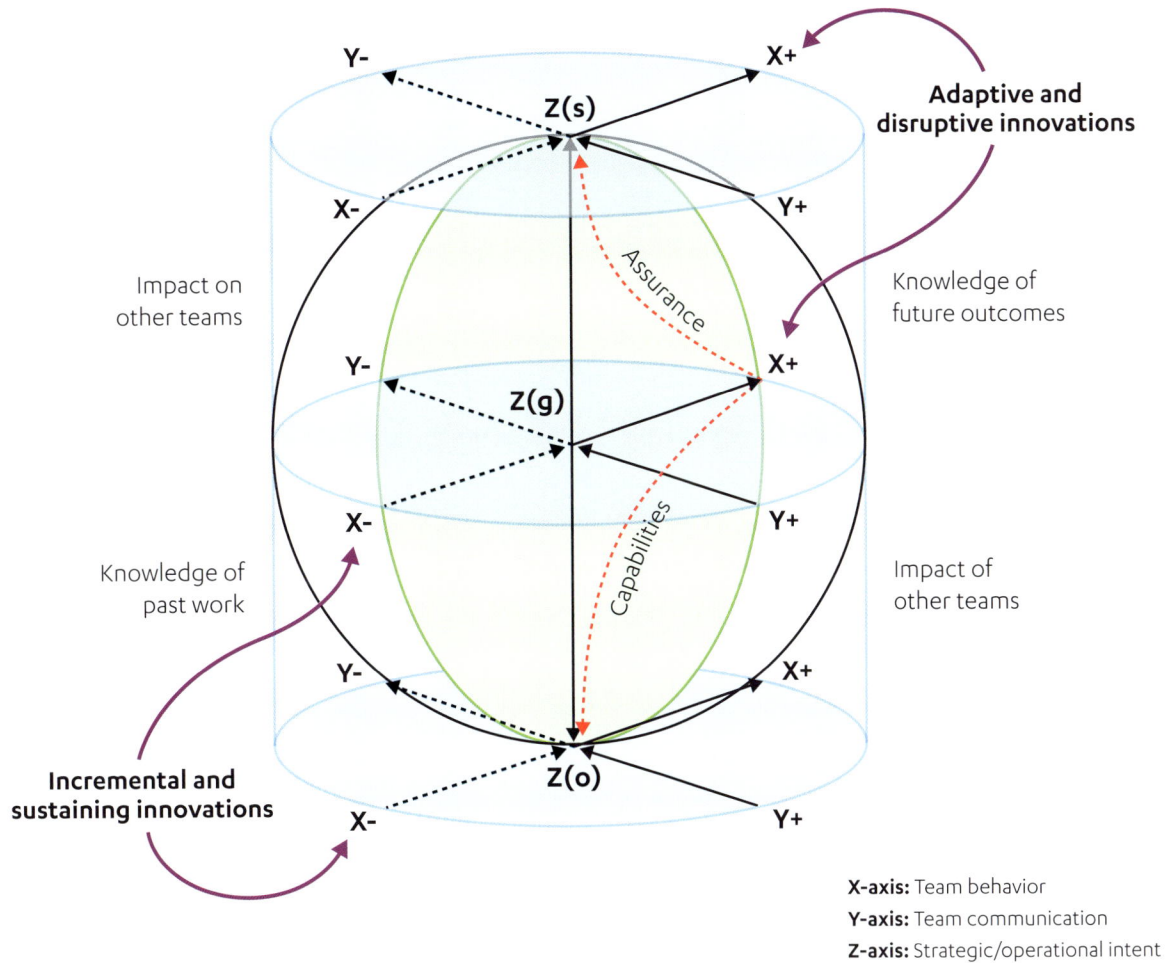

Figure 7.1 The 3D Knowledge Model

It is advantageous to work in an environment where you understand what you are doing and why it is essential to the organization. You comprehend the work you do and the value your efforts add. You also know what other teams expect and continually keep everyone productively apprised of their work. The 3D Knowledge Model is not limited to internal use, and can also be applied to partner and supplier contracts (for example, the top and bottom "layers"; see section 3.1.2).

7.3 Decision-making and systems thinking

Decision-making in a CAS requires understanding the type of problem (performance gap) under study. Obviously, simple problems are simple, but complicated problems are not complex. In this section, we'll discuss how organizations can use Cynefin as a decision-making tool and how it complements the DVMS Z-X Model's four aspects of innovation. We'll cover the importance of Cynefin's power as a decision-making tool, and its role in helping an organization as it works *on* and *in* its DVMS.

7.3.1 Decision-making with Cynefin

The Cynefin framework (Figure 5.1) is a helpful tool for decision-making. David J. Snowden created it in 1999 while working for IBM Global Services. The framework is named after the Welsh word for "habitat." It gives decision-makers a "sense of place" to assess their perceptions of performance gaps.

The Cynefin framework includes five decision-making contexts or "domains": clear, complicated, complex, chaotic, and a center of confusion. These domains assist managers in identifying how they perceive situations and understanding their own and other people's behavior. The framework is based on research into systems, complexity, networks, and learning theories.

The domains on the right-hand side, clear and complicated, are "ordered," where cause and effect are known or easily discovered. Those on the left-hand side, complex and chaotic, are "unordered," where cause and effect can be determined only with hindsight or not at all. The Cynefin framework offers a structured approach to decision-making that can provide a helpful perspective on complex situations.

In problem-solving, the **clear domain** is where the situation is stable and clear cause-and-effect relationships exist. It represents the "known knowns," where rules and best practices are established. To tackle such cases, one should follow a "sense-categorize-respond" approach: first gather the facts ("sense"), then categorize them, and then respond by looking backward to well-established rules or best practices.

The **complicated domain** includes situations that are uncertain but not entirely unknown. Understanding the cause and effect requires analysis or expertise, and there may be multiple correct solutions. To navigate this domain, the recommended approach is to "sense-analyze-respond." This means evaluating the facts, analyzing them, and applying good practices appropriate for the situation. It's similar to an engineering exercise, where you work within a familiar framework but with complicated variables and behaviors.

The **complex domain** is a realm of uncertainty where it's difficult to determine cause and effect. It's full of "unknown unknowns," and there are no clear-cut solutions. According to Snowden, organizational leaders can learn from this domain by safely experimenting with different approaches. This process, known as "probe-sense-respond," can help reveal instructive patterns. Examples of complex systems include markets, ecosystems, and corporate cultures. These systems resist reductionist approaches because any action can result in unpredictable changes, throwing the system into chaos.

In the **chaotic domain**, it can be difficult to determine cause and effect. Situations in this domain are often too complex to wait for a response based on knowledge alone. Therefore, it is necessary to act – taking any action – as the initial and only appropriate response. In such cases, managers generally adopt the approach of "act-sense-respond": taking action to bring about order, sensing where to find stability, and responding to transform the chaotic into the complex.

When in the chaotic domain, leadership's priority is to stop bleeding. Leaders must take action to bring order, and then assess where stability exists and where it is lacking. From there, they must work to transform the situation from chaos to complexity. This allows them to identify emerging patterns to prevent future crises and uncover new opportunities. The DVMS 3D Knowledge Model plays a vital role in supporting this effort. The organization must stabilize its situation before optimizing its current capabilities and pursuing ongoing innovation.

The central area of the framework represents the **confusion domain**, where there is no clear application of the other domains. Identifying when this domain applies can be challenging, as it involves multiple perspectives and conflicting arguments among factional leaders. One approach breaks down the situation into its constituent parts and assigns each to one of the other four realms. This allows leaders to make informed decisions and intervene appropriately according to the context, thereby finding a way out of this domain.

7.3.2 Decision-making: Working *on* and *in* a system

Once the organization has determined the nature of the performance gaps, it can choose the appropriate points to apply leverage according to which domain it is in:

- **Clear** Clear gaps in performance can be quickly resolved within the framework of established best practices. Such changes to organizational capabilities usually constitute incremental innovations and are addressed through the Governance/Execution loop of the DVMS CPD Model. These types of improvements are made within the constraints set by policies

- **Complicated** Determining the extent of innovation becomes more complicated when many variables are at play. However, it still falls within established policy constraints. Depending on the level of innovation, either the Governance/Execution or the Strategy/Governance loop of the DVMS CPD Model might be the appropriate point of application

- **Complex** Complex problems involve enabling constraints such as policy or strategy. Often, in a CAS, emergent or unforeseen practices occur. These problems require adaptive changes to policy or disruptive changes to strategy. This type of innovation is handled in the Strategy/Governance loop of the DVMS CPD Model

- **Chaotic** During chaotic situations, leaders must take action and observe the system's response to determine the type of problem at hand. It's crucial to stop any damage from escalating. Leaders may sometimes need to consider various perspectives from complex, complicated, and clear domains to understand the issue holistically

- **Confusion** This domain applies when there is no clear-cut association with the other domains. Resolving this situation requires decomposing the "confusion" into constituent parts that can be appropriately classified.

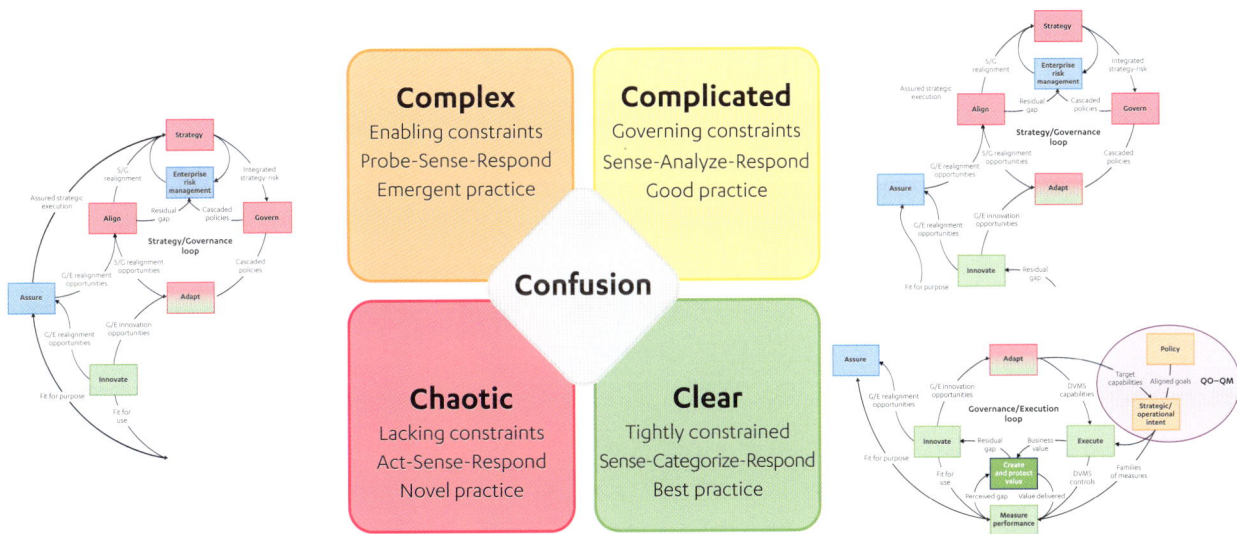

Figure 7.2 The DVMS CPD Model and Cynefin

7.4 Chapter takeaways

This chapter ties a lot of things together within the context of the DVMS. The ideas presented in the previous chapters are repurposed with a specific DVMS context.

CHAPTER 8
Gaining a new perspective

8 Gaining a new perspective

We started this journey with a discussion about the significance of thinking differently and changing our perspective to look at things from a new viewpoint. Just as it would be challenging for someone living in a two-dimensional world to imagine height, our thinking can also be restricted by the limitations of our surroundings. We reviewed Senge's laws of mental models (section 3.1.1), which suggest that human beings tend to think in the same way because those ideas have historically been effective. However, just because a particular solution has worked before, that does not mean it will always work: we must be open to new ways of thinking and adapting to change. In other words, "Things work right up to the point where they don't."

The genius behind Senge's writing is that he made systems thinking easier for everyone to understand. His "laws" are more like principles: immutable but still subject to abuse. Systems thinking is at the core of our journey and shaped our thinking about the DVMS CPD Model. We needed a way to explain how a business, modeled as a CAS, described how organizations work in the natural world. It provides a simple way to think about the complexities of our organizations, from a one-person shop to a multi-million-person international business. It also provides a way to think differently about how our organization functions and helps provide insight into how leverage impacts its behaviors.

When you apply systems thinking, you gain a new perspective, which can often inspire you to approach problems differently. Meadows' writings teach us that the most effective way to alter how a system behaves is to step outside of it and change its paradigm. To think differently is to break away from your current approach to managing digital value and envision a new one that actively creates, safeguards, and delivers digital value to all stakeholders.

The beautiful thing about systems, particularly CAS, is that they always self-organize around their paradigm. The DVMS CPD Model is a systems archetype representing how businesses survive and thrive in chaotic environments. It's based on Senge's "laws" and embodies Meadows' 12 leverage points (sections 3.3 and 5.2.2) to coax a CAS into a desired set of behaviors.

8.1 The new normal

The DVMS CPD Model operationalizes the DVMS Z-X Model, representing the minimal viable capabilities an organization *must* possess to create, protect, and deliver digital business value to its stakeholders. Each capability provides the practice areas, practices, and outcomes necessary to achieve that. Its focus is on outcomes, not process, because of what we discussed with Cynefin: clear problems are best addressed with best practices. However, the other problems you'll encounter will require a deeper understanding; solutions must be formulated within the guidance provided by the tolerances associated with organizational policy. We learned that complexity isn't complicated, and often requires a different approach that may include changes to policy or strategy. This is described in the DVMS CPD Model and its operationalization of the DVMS Z-X Model (section 2.3.2).

We realized that to start making any change, we had to start where we are. While that sounds condescending, it's human nature (and part of Senge's laws) that people will fall back on what they know and seek a familiar starting point that isn't where they are. The starting point, in reality, is where you are assessed to be. That becomes your baseline, and now we can talk about why we called this section the "new normal."

The DVMS CPD Model is centered around the idea of how an organization can survive and thrive in a naturally chaotic environment. This means that being able to adapt and change must become a critical capability for the organization. Through experimentation, it can learn its natural rhythm for making and absorbing changes. This process involves working both *on* the system (making changes to capabilities) and *in* it (utilizing those capabilities to produce outcomes). With every innovation that impacts the system, there is a period of adjustment before it becomes the "new normal" condition from which the next innovation will be made. It's important to note that in the DVMS, the "new normal" is never an endpoint or the last change. Change must be constant in the DVMS to ensure that performance gaps are minimized according to the organizational policies.

8.2   The learning organization

In his book *The Fifth Discipline*, Peter Senge (2006) discusses the concept of systems thinking and how it can help an organization become a "learning organization." However, from our experience, we have learned that the key to fostering a learning organization is to empower individuals within the organization to pursue personal mastery. An environment that encourages cross-team learning is crucial for creating a learning organization. According to Senge, team learning involves three essential aspects:

- Developing insightful thinking about complex issues
- Taking innovative and coordinated action
- Creating a network that enables other teams to act.

The DVMS 3D Knowledge Model is an excellent example of a structure that promotes transparency and eliminates information or knowledge silos. By working together, teams can learn, adapt, and improve.

The organizational capability to create, protect, and deliver digital business value to stakeholders relies heavily on the capacity to learn. This may seem like an obvious statement, but it actually describes how a learning organization functions. As it gains knowledge about a problem, it also learns more about the solution, and as it gains knowledge about the solution, it also learns more about the problem. This cycle is the essence of a learning organization, characterized by its ability to continually seek out better solutions.

8.3   The DVMS as an overlay

The DVMS is an overlay. That means that an adopting organization can use it to overlay its existing capabilities and surface the performance gaps that prevent it from being able to create, protect, and deliver digital business value to its stakeholders with assurance. Now, it's one thing to say you can do something and a totally different thing to prove it.

The DVMS Z-X Model provides a full description of a minimal set of capabilities an organization must have to say it can create, protect, and deliver digital business value *and prove it*. The DVMS, operationalized by the DVMS Z-X Model, enables an organization to create value and ensure it's appropriately protected and delivered to stakeholders. It does not replace the frameworks and methods currently in use, but provides the organization with something to measure its capabilities against. It's not a framework or a method; it's not about the processes you use to achieve your outcomes: it's a scalable-and-adaptable-by-all approach to achieving a new organizational paradigm (see Figure 8.1).

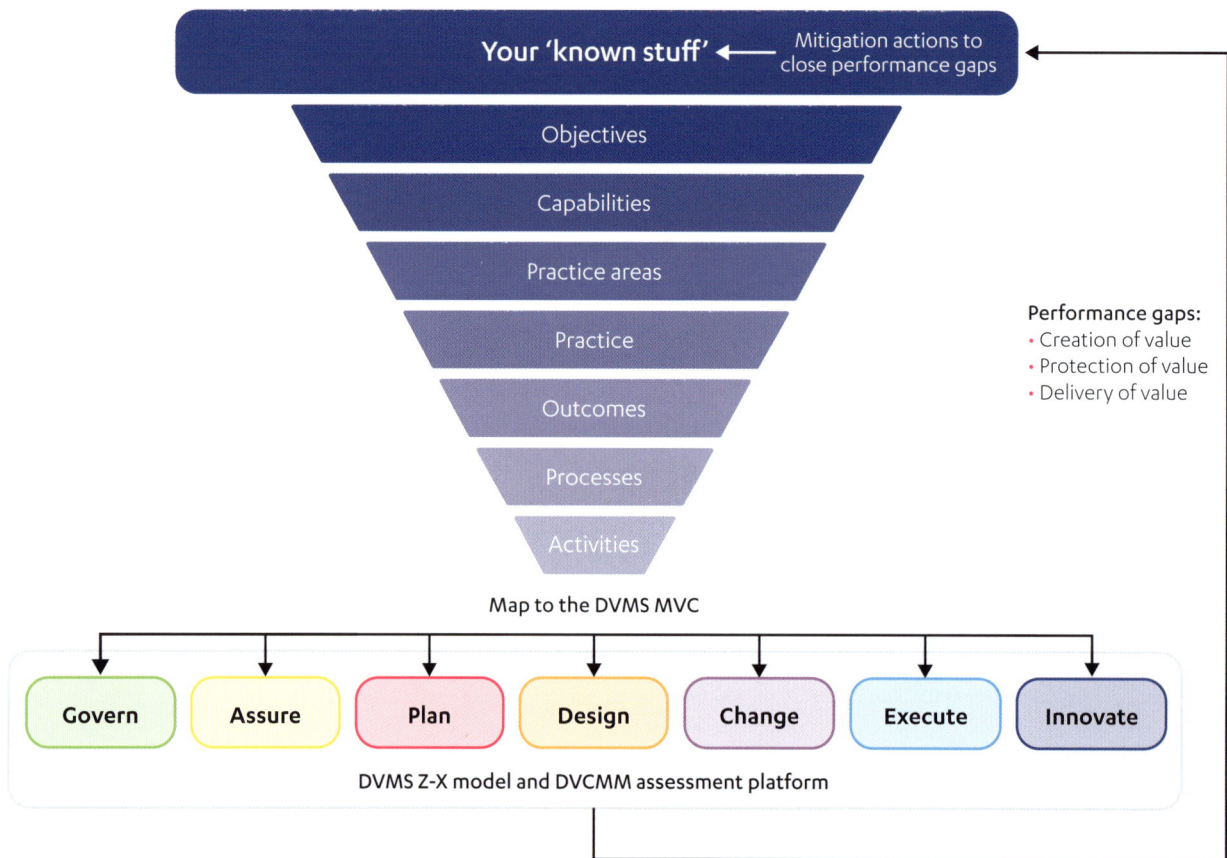

Figure 8.1 How your stuff fits the DVMS MVC

8.4   Chapter takeaways

We began this book with this quote from Dr. Wayne Dyer: "If you change the way you look at things, the things you look at change." We've tried to give you a different way to look at organizations in the context of a system to help you understand what it entails to build a learning organization with a learning culture that is resilient and able to respond to changes, whether internal or external, quickly.

Thank you for reading.

APPENDIX A:
DVMS practice areas

Appendix A: DVMS practice areas

Within the DVMS context, the MVC provides a grouping of practices that we call "practice areas," which in turn decompose into individual "practices." It is an organizational responsibility to define the processes that bring these practices to life and execute the associated tasks and activities. This approach supports DVMS scalability an outcomes scale based on organizational growth and resources.

Governance operating model

The DVMS Z-X Model enables organizations to implement effective Govern and Assure capabilities. The focus is on the Governance/Assurance loop within the CPD Model, a subset of a broader governance operating model. At a high level, a typical governance operating model covers the following areas: organizational design and reporting structure, oversight responsibilities, talent and culture, infrastructure such as policies and procedures, transparency in reporting, and digital business value; and it addresses the following:

- Structure
  - Organizational design and reporting structure
  - Organizational structure and charters
- Oversight responsibilities
  - Organizational oversight and responsibilities
  - Management accountability and authority
  - Committee accountability, authorities, and responsibilities
- Talent and culture
  - Performance management and incentives
  - Business and operating principles
  - Leadership development and talent programs
- Infrastructure
  - Policies and procedures
  - Transparency in reporting and communication
  - Digital business value.

The following two sections (A.1 and A.2) examine organizational capabilities based on COSO ERM principles. It's crucial to understand the organizational governance structure's scope, including the board of directors' role in management, and how the DVMS Z-X Model implements the Govern and Assure capabilities.

A.1 Govern (GO)

The DVMS Z-X Model is a way to implement governance, similar to bootstrapping governance. In the CPD Model's Governance/Assurance loop, the Govern capability is related to strategy-risk, which leads to organizational objectives. These objectives are then translated into management policies that help create, protect, and deliver digital business value. The board sets the rules and goals for the system, while management establishes the business objectives to achieve those goals. Policies provide guidance to improve organizational capabilities and ensure desired system behaviors. In the DVMS Z-X Model's Govern capability, there are three practice areas:

- **Identify critical business systems** Determine what is valuable
- **Establish digital business risk posture** Decide at what level to protect the value
- **Oversee DVMS performance** Instrument warranty and utility of the DVMS capabilities.

GO:1 – Identify critical business systems practice area

The top management team pinpoints the critical business systems, not IT systems or applications, that provide value to stakeholders. These organizational capabilities that create business value and support digital assets are part of the business system. The organization can then distribute and arrange the business value its digital assets make possible. As the organization becomes more adaptable, it must consistently evaluate the value generated for its stakeholders, considering internal organizational demands, external demands, and an ever-changing threat environment. New business systems will be established, and older ones will be updated or retired.

GO:2 – Establish digital business risk posture practice area

In this area, the goal is to determine the best way to manage risk for the organization. This involves evaluating the organizational ability to safeguard digital assets against internal and external threats. The organization thoroughly assesses its capabilities and determines its optimal risk posture. It must answer the question: "How much risk can we take on?"

While the available resources may limit the organizational ability to implement a risk-based approach to cybersecurity, cost is not the only factor considered. The organization makes informed decisions about its risk mitigation strategy. Its ultimate goal is to prioritize and protect critical business systems while optimizing its risk posture.

GO:3 – Oversee DVMS performance practice area

This practice area is responsible for turning the organizational risk-informed business strategy (strategy-risk) into business objectives. The result is a cascading set of policies that provide management guidance for creating or improving the organizational capabilities to create, protect, and deliver digital business value for stakeholders. This practice area includes the alignment of outcomes of the business objectives, and the subsequent expression of strategic and operational intent (SOI) as measures and metrics used to identify performance gaps.

The board sets the rules and goals for the system management, organizes them to conform to them, and works to see the established goals being realized. An integral part of this requires ensuring the correct instrumentation of the organizational capabilities to produce the measures and metrics required to assure performance and tie the Governance/Assurance loop together at "Measure performance" (Figure 2.5).

A.2 Assure (AS)

The DVMS Z-X Model's Assure capability gives the organization confidence in executing its strategic policies. The resultant organizational capabilities provide the appropriate level of warranty and utility (fitness for use and purpose) that the organization requires. The Govern and Assure capabilities mesh with performance measurement in the Governance/Assurance loop. While the Govern capability establishes the objectives and how the organization will achieve them, Assure "proves" that the appropriate innovation authority has addressed performance gaps.

In the DVMS Z-X Model's Assure capability, there are four practice areas:

- **Establish assurance criteria** Instrument warranty and utility of the DVMS capabilities
- **Assure strategic policy performance** Identify performance gaps in the execution of strategic policy
- **Assure operational capability** Identify performance gaps relative to fitness and use
- **Assure performance measurement accuracy** Identify gaps in the accuracy of the SOI schema.

AS:1 – Establish assurance criteria practice area

This area of practice complements the oversight of DVMS performance practice area (GO:3). However, it focuses on establishing an "assurance point of view" for the instrumentation of organizational capabilities. AS:1 and GO:3 work together to determine the measurements and metrics used to ensure that the organizational capabilities fit their intended use and purpose. The Govern perspective ensures that the capabilities created or improved are designed as intended, while Assure verifies that they produce the desired outcomes effectively and efficiently. These different viewpoints result in various measures and metrics. The SOI determines the measures and metrics used to instrument the organizational capabilities. Performance measurement then uses these measures and metrics to identify any performance gaps.

AS:2 – Assure strategic policy performance practice area

Strategic policy performance measures gaps in organizational capabilities to follow the rules and goals established by strategy-risk. It measures the adaptation of the strategic policies to create or improve organizational capabilities to produce the desired business outcomes. The performance gaps generally reflect the residual capabilities achieved as the organization creates or improves existing capabilities. This is particularly important in an adaptive organization as it continually delivers incremental improvements to organizational capabilities. Even then, there will still be tweaks within the design tolerance of the system established by policy. Do not think of a performance gap as a failure; treat it as an indicator of progress toward a business objective.

AS:3 – Assure operational capability practice area

Like AS:2, this practice identifies performance gaps in organizational capabilities at the operational level. At this level, operational performance gaps determine whether organizational capabilities to produce the desired outcomes conform to the design and are effective and efficient. The appropriate innovation authority acts to address performance gaps. However, all changes represent low-order leverage points within the system. An organization can tweak performance within its tolerances established by strategic and operational policies.

AS:4 – Assure performance measurement accuracy practice area

Performance measurement uses measures and metrics that express the organizational SOI – "what we want to do and how." These measures and metrics are derived from the QO–QM capability of the Governance/Assurance loop and instrumented within the organizational capabilities. If the measures and metrics are wrong, decisions made from that information may not be correct or effective.

A.3   Plan (PL)

The Plan capability enables the organization to govern, assure performance, create and execute a risk-informed business strategy, and manage its portfolio of programs, risks, and projects, and organizational knowledge. The practice areas of the Plan capability subsequently enable the organization to create, protect, and deliver digital business value.

The purpose of the Plan capability subsumes two goals: to create and deliver digital business value, and to protect that delivered value at a level commensurate with its significance to the business.

There are five practice areas under the Plan capability:

- Governance
- Assurance
- Strategy-risk management
- Portfolio, program, and project management
- Knowledge management.

PL:1 – Governance practice area

Governance is "the act or process of governing or overseeing the control and direction of something (such as a country or an organization)" (*The Merriam-Webster Dictionary*). The DVMS Z-X Model's governance practice area defines the organizational structure (the who does what to whom, when, and why) and formulates the policies for the organization to work. The practice area has two practices:

PL:1-1 Create organizational structures

This practice aims to develop an organizational structure to create, protect, and deliver digital business value. It's based on the principle that behavior and structure are inextricably linked. The resultant structure aligns with the organizational SOI.

PL:1-2 Sustain organizational structures

Every system or structure tends toward disorganization. This practice examines and improves the organizational digital business risk culture and its resulting behaviors to sustain the organizational capability to create, protect, and deliver digital business value. It seeks to operationalize a structure that aligns with the organizational SOI.

PL:2 – Assurance practice area

The *Merriam-Webster Dictionary* defines "assurance" as "confidence of mind or manner: easy freedom from self-doubt or uncertainty." The DVMS assurance practice area provides confidence that organizational strategic policies are executed efficiently and effectively; it also provides assurance that the DVMS capabilities are fit for use and purpose, and that the value created is protected at a level commensurate with its importance to the organization. Overall, this practice area seeks to identify performance gaps, assess them, and communicate them to stakeholders.

PL:2-1 Performance assurance

The performance assurance practice seeks to identify the measures and metrics necessary to provide assurance that policies align with the organizational SOI. It aims to align organizational goals to create, protect, and deliver digital business value.

PL:2-2 Review and revision

Continual innovation is a core organizational capability; this practice seeks to identify improvement opportunities for the DVMS capabilities and strategic policy realignment. It subsequently communicates validated improvement opportunities to the change coordination practice for assessment and action.

PL:2-3 Information sharing and reporting

This practice creates a reporting framework that supports the CPD Model's capability to assure the stakeholders that strategic policies are executed efficiently and effectively and that DVMS capabilities are fit for use and purpose. The reporting framework includes a stakeholder information-sharing plan and provides a comprehensive report on the current state of the CPD Model.

PL:3 – Strategy-risk management practice area

This practice area aggregates the practices that integrate the strategy-risk policies into the DVMS: strategy-risk policy execution, identifying improvement opportunities, planning, testing continuity plans, and oversight of the supply chain cybersecurity posture. These activities support creating resilience and accountability, and provide the basis for adaptive and disruptive innovation by defining performance tolerances – one result of making strategy-risk a single entity.

PL:3-1 Policy integration

The DVMS is how policies become actionable business objectives that create, protect, and deliver digital business value. The strategy-risk policies adapt the DVMS capabilities to effectively and efficiently execute policies.

PL:3-2 Identify improvement opportunities

The dynamic nature of the CPD Model enables it to adapt to a changing organizational context, including the realignment of strategy-risk policies. Evaluate performance gaps for opportunities to improve (realign) strategy-risk policies.

PL:3-3 Digital business continuity management

Businesses rely on digital assets to contribute to business value. The combination of strategy and risk into a single entity, strategy-risk, includes resilience in the form of digital business value continuity. This practice ensures the business has a tested plan that is verified and capable of supporting the business's recovery in the event of a severe incident.

PL:3-4 Supply chain risk management

No business in this interconnected business world stands alone. Digital business systems connect with suppliers and businesses to supply goods or services. Everyone is connected to everyone else. *This connectedness creates a complex problem for the organization: its cybersecurity posture is only as strong as the posture of its weakest supplier.* The associated processes of this practice seek to manage third-party provider risk and give assurance that those providers demonstrate a cybersecurity profile that supports achieving the desired organizational risk posture.

PL:4 – Portfolio, program, and project management practice area

This practice area is involved in two aspects of the DVMS to provide the structural capacity to:

- Implement or improve the DVMS capabilities
- Manage the DVMS capabilities, practice areas, and practices to create, protect, and deliver digital business value.

The practice area focuses on organizational values and protection needs. This focus gives the organization an objective measure to make critical resource decisions.

PL:4-1 Establish digital business value portfolio

This practice establishes and maintains a portfolio that provides visibility of the organizational offerings that create, protect, and deliver digital business value. It catalogs offerings and communicates value and risk performance. The objective information is used for everyday and critical business and resource decisions.

PL:4-2 Program and project management

This practice aggregates one or more related projects that apply the knowledge, skills, and tools to facilitate the introduction of change. It efficiently manages one or more projects and effectively manages the activities that introduce change.

PL:5 – Knowledge management practice area

Knowledge management is the practice of creating, sharing, using, and managing organizational knowledge. It is a multidisciplinary approach to support decisions that achieve objectives using knowledge.

Let's look at the data, information, knowledge, and wisdom (DIKW) model and put that in context for the CPD Model and this DVMS practice area.

The DIKW model

The DIKW model (Figure A.1) is typically represented as a pyramid (Rowley, 2007), with **data** forming its base. Data has no meaning until the application of a transform provides context; then, it becomes **information** that answers questions like "who," "what," "when," and "where." The application of additional transforms provides additional meaning; information becomes **knowledge**, answering the question of "how." Combined, data, information, and knowledge reveal questions and potential answers about relationships and patterns of behaviors over time that contribute to **wisdom**, resulting in better decisions – answering the question of "why." Purposely, decisions result in changes (adaptive or disruptive innovation).

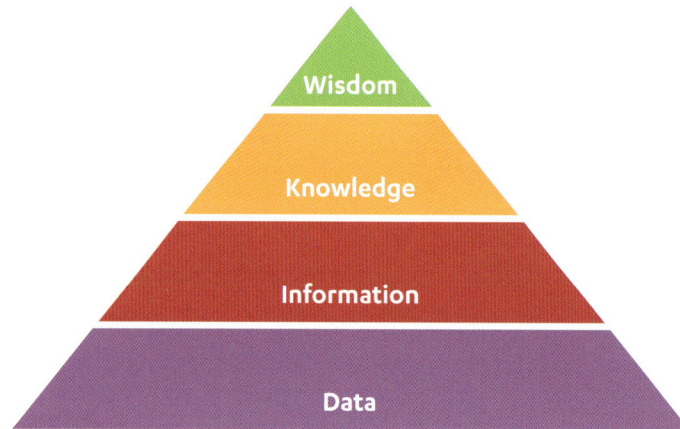

```
        Wisdom
      Knowledge
    Information
      Data
```

Figure A.1 The DIKW model

Knowledge management model

The output of strategy-risk is risk-informed strategic policies. These policies are adapted to produce the DVMS control requirements necessary to create, protect, and deliver digital business value. The QO–QM method uses strategic policies and the desired DVMS capabilities to align strategic outcomes and produce the metrics and measures that express the organizational SOI. QO–QM output metrics are used to instrument the DVMS practice and develop the SOI schema. The SOI schema maps the data collected in various data stores by operating the DVMS practices to determine performance gaps in the DVMS operation and execution of strategic policies.

The information provides assurance that the DVMS capabilities are performing within tolerances and that policies are being executed effectively and efficiently. These two feedback loops allow the organization to improve continually relative to its environment. This method of innovation is considered to be adaptive.

Similarly, an innovation that results in a paradigm shift is assessed and actioned within the CPD Model's Strategy/ Governance loop and in corresponding changes to strategy-risk and cascaded strategic policies.

PL:5-1 Manage the flow of information

One of the three "flows" fundamental to any organization is the flow of information. This practice aims to create, share, use, and manage organizational information and knowledge. It seeks to leverage information and knowledge to help achieve organizational objectives.

PL:5-2 Audit and manage the information lifecycle

Information is only as good as the data it's based on and the understanding of its context. This practice aims to verify and validate information and knowledge to provide assurance that organizational objectives are achieved. It aims to produce verifiable and validated information and knowledge to support organizational objectives.

PL:5-3 Manage stakeholder information flow

This practice seeks to manage the flow of information that stakeholders use to achieve organizational goals. It provides the correct information to the right stakeholder at the right place and time.

A.4 Design (DE)

The Design capability enables the organization to create a straightforward, cohesive approach to creating, protecting, and delivering digital business value. It seeks to develop designs through the system architecture and configuration management practice areas that enable the organization to create and deliver appropriately protected digital business value.

There are two practice areas under the Design capability:

- System architecture
- Configuration management.

DE:1 – System architecture practice area

The system architecture practice area covers practices that support the organizational ability to create clear and cohesive designs to create, protect, and deliver digital business value.

DE:1-1 Performance management

The performance management practice develops and maintains the architectural plans that describe the organizational structure, relationships, interaction pattern, and environment to create, protect, and deliver digital business value. It delivers architectural plans that describe the creation, protection, and delivery of digital business value to assure conformance to architectural plans.

DE:1-2 Availability management

Availability management establishes the scope and tolerances of the operational availability of digital assets that create, protect, and deliver digital business value. The scope and tolerances include availability, reliability, maintainability, and continuity relative to the architectural performance management criteria.

DE:1-3 Capacity management

Capacity management establishes the scope and tolerances of the operational performance of digital assets that create, protect, and deliver digital business value. The scope and tolerances include operational performance relative to the architectural performance management criteria.

DE:1-4 Continuity management

Continuity management develops architectural plans to ensure business continuity when responding to a serious incident. These plans are reviewed, verified, and validated to assure the organization that the plans support sufficient business recovery in such a situation.

DE:2 – Configuration management practice area

Configuration management is essential in the organizational ability to associate digital assets with the systems that create, protect, and deliver digital business value. Configuration management defines the scope, including linkages to business value and assessment against the SOI.

DE:2-1 Configuration item management

Configuration item management establishes the scope and relationships of the configuration items managed in conformance with the system architecture. It logically represents the configuration item attributes and relationships contributing to digital business value creation, protection, and delivery.

DE:2-2 Configuration administration

Configuration administration establishes the scope of the administrative control over configuration items, and ensures conformance with the system architecture and digital business value. Conformance with the architecture ensures retention of the relationship and interaction patterns that are part of the architecture. The practice represents the configuration items to reflect their physical and virtual manifestation.

A.5   Change (CH)

Change is a fundamental organizational capability that enables an organization to adapt to its environment. Internal and external needs and a dynamic threat environment drive the Change capability. It affects digital solutions that meet the design requirements necessary to create, protect, and deliver digital business value. It establishes the governance structure essential to coordinate digital business value solutions.

There are four practice areas under the Change capability:

- Change coordination
- Solution adaptation
- Release management
- Deployment management.

CH:1 – Change coordination practice area

The change coordination practice area aggregates the organizational orchestration of how change impacts people, practice, technology, and risk. It provides overarching governance that involves the organizational authorized change authorities, stakeholders, and stakeholder relationships, and coordinates the selection, build, release, and deployment of changes to digital products, services, and systems.

CH:1-1 Change orchestration

The change orchestration practice ensures the coordination of the authorization to build, release, and deploy changes to digital products, services, and systems to create, protect, and deliver digital business value.

CH:1-2 Performance assessment

The performance assessment practice ensures that each implementation of a change is assessed against the expected value expressed in the SOI. It provides assurance that each implemented change creates, protects, and delivers digital business value aligned with the SOI.

CH:2 – Solution adaptation practice area

The solution adaptation practice area is tightly integrated with change coordination, configuration management, and system architecture. These practices are core to the *creation* of digital business. The organization *must* be at DVCMM level 3 to provide the necessary capability to integrate dependent informative reference control requirements into the DVMS practices. The relationship between the DVMS capabilities and the informative reference control families (to the level of the individual control requirements) is critical and must not be overlooked or underestimated.

This practice area aggregates the adaptation of commercial solutions, digital hardware, software, something as a service (XaaS), and performance assessment.

CH:2-1 Commercial solution acquisition

This practice ensures that acquiring hardware, software, and services aligns with the organizational SOI to create, protect, and deliver digital business value by establishing the acquisition criteria.

CH:2-2 Digital hardware solution

The digital hardware solution practice ensures that the installation, integration, and removal of digital hardware align with the organizational SOI to create, protect, and deliver digital business value.

CH:2-3 Software solution

The software solution practice ensures that software installation, integration, and removal align with the organizational SOI to create, protect, and deliver digital business value.

CH:2-4 XaaS solution

The XaaS solution practice ensures that the installation, integration, and removal of XaaS solutions align with the organizational SOI to create, protect, and deliver digital business value.

CH:2-5 Performance assessment

The performance assessment practice looks at adapting solutions based on the expected value expressed in the organizational SOI. It ensures the adapted solution creates, protects, and delivers digital business value aligned with the organizational SOI.

CH:3 – Release management practice area

The release management practice area aggregates the planning of a release, monitoring its build and testing, and comprehensive testing of the entire release.

CH:3-1 Release planning

Release planning encompasses developing an actionable plan to release, independent of size, an identified set of components into the live environment to create, protect, and deliver digital business value. It identifies and sources the components to be released together.

CH:3-2 Monitor component build and test

This practice ensures that the build and testing of all release components are monitored throughout the build-and-test cycle, with release plans being kept up to date, including component build and testing results.

CH:3-3 Release testing

This practice develops and executes a release test plan to provide assurance that the release conforms with the SOI. The executable test plan helps to ensure that the release achieves the SOI to create, protect, and deliver digital business value.

CH:4 – Deployment management practice area

The deployment management practice area manages the deployment of the release package into, or decommissioning from, the live environment and validates the result.

CH:4-1 Manage release transition

The manage release transition practice deals with adding or decommissioning functionality that aligns with the organizational SOI. It adds approved release packages, or removes decommission-approved functionality that is no longer needed to create, protect, and deliver digital business value.

CH:4-2 Validate

The validation practice provides assurance that the addition or decommissioning of functionality is aligned with the organizational SOI to create, protect, and deliver digital business value.

A.6   Execute (EX)

The Execute capability is where created and protected value is delivered. Its practice areas encompass providing access to digital products, services, and systems to authorized users; mitigating disruptions in the delivery of digital business value; identifying and resolving system disruption of digital business value; and managing the organizational infrastructure/platforms.

The Execute capability has four practice areas:

- Provisioning
- Productivity management
- Problem management
- Infrastructure/platform management.

EX:1 – Provisioning practice area

The provisioning practice area aggregates the practices that manage access to digital products, services, and systems. It also deals with access requests.

EX:1-1 Access management

The access management practice establishes and maintains policies to determine who (or what) is authorized to have access to digital products, services, and systems. It executes these policies in alignment with the organizational SOI.

EX:1-2 Request management

The request management practice maintains authorized access to digital products, services, and systems in alignment with the organizational SOI.

EX:2 – Productivity management practice area

The productivity management practice area develops and maintains incident models that support restoring business productivity in response to incidents, in alignment with the organizational SOI to create, protect, and deliver digital business value.

EX:2-1 Manage incident models

The manage incident models practice develops and maintains incident models to support the restoration of business productivity. The incident models enable the organization to restore business productivity in a timeframe aligned with the organizational SOI.

EX:2-2 Execute incident model

The execute incident model practice applies and executes an appropriate incident model that restores business productivity in a timeframe aligned with the organizational SOI.

EX:3 – Problem management practice area

The problem management practice area defines problem models and their selection criteria, and executes them to remove systemic errors from digital products, services, and systems.

EX:3-1 Manage problem models

The problem management practice defines and executes an appropriate problem model that supports identifying and removing system errors in digital products, services, and systems in alignment with the organizational SOI to create, protect, and deliver digital business value.

EX:3-2 Execute problem model

The execute problem model practice applies the model execution in identifying and removing systemic errors in digital products, services, and systems, or developing workarounds in alignment with the organizational SOI.

EX:4 – Infrastructure/platform management practice area

This practice area aggregates practices that monitor and manage infrastructure events.

EX:4-1 Event monitoring

Event monitoring ensures the identification of events with the coordination, instrumentation, and monitoring provisions aligned with the organizational SOI to create, protect, and deliver digital business value.

EX:4-2 Event management

The event management practice identifies, correlates, and responds to events in alignment with the organizational SOI to create, protect, and deliver digital business value.

A.7   Innovate (IN)

The DVMS Model overlays organizational capabilities that represent a minimum viable capability necessary to create, protect, and deliver digital business value. It assumes the organization is at some unknown capability state when the model is used, marking the beginning of the organizational journey.

The organization starts "where it is." That means anything the organization does is considered an innovation. Innovation is the introduction of something new. The DVMS operationalizes the CPD Model. The CPD Model enables an organization to continually adapt to its current context through incremental or sustaining changes. It also incorporates an organizational capability to operationalize changes representing either a paradigm shift or disruption in the marketplace.

The Innovate capability seeks opportunities to innovate in creating, protecting, and delivering digital business value to achieve the organizational SOI. It measures the overall performance of the components and systems that create, protect, and deliver digital business value, analyzes performance gaps, and catalogs innovation opportunities.

Much like a flywheel in a car engine provides mass that keeps the engine turning, continual innovation keeps the DVMS capabilities adapting to the dynamic organizational environment.

The Innovate capability has three practice areas:

- Continual innovation
- Performance measurement
- Gap analysis.

IN:1 – Continual innovation practice area

Internal and external changes and a dynamic threat landscape provide the incremental impetus to improve continually. In this model, the Innovate capability identifies improvement types, recording, and notification to a change authority. The change coordination practice area is responsible for effecting the change. The results reflect capabilities, policies, and SOI updates.

IN:1-1 Innovation management

Innovation management promotes the systematic renewal and innovation of organizational capabilities that create, protect, and deliver digital business value. It creates and uses innovation models.

IN:1-2 Model innovation types

This practice develops and maintains improvement models representing innovation opportunities that are consistent with the SOI to create, protect, and deliver digital business value. These models represent the types of innovation.

IN:1-3 Use innovation models

This practice applies the appropriate innovation model to assess, record, and notify a change authority of an innovation opportunity that conforms to the SOI to create, protect, and deliver digital business value.

IN:2 – Performance measurement practice area

The performance measurement practice area is responsible for the instrumentation of the DVMS practices so their performance can be assessed against the organizational SOI and the delivery of expected digital business value. The measures and metrics derived from the SOI are used to develop and maintain the DVMS reporting schema.

IN:2-1 Instrument practice outcomes

This practice ensures that DVMS practices are instrumented to identify the alignment of the SOI in order to create, protect, and deliver digital business value.

IN:2-2 DVMS reporting

This practice develops and maintains a DVMS reporting schema for the instrumented practices in alignment with the SOI to create, protect, and deliver digital business value. The DVMS reporting schema provides visibility into alignment with the SOI.

IN:3 – Gap analysis practice area

This practice area develops and uses models to assess the gaps in the performance of the DVMS capabilities to create, protect, and deliver digital business value.

IN:3-1 Determine the gap

This practice determines whether an out-of-tolerance condition exists between the current state and the organizational SOI to create, protect, and deliver digital business value. The activities related to this practice require teams working in the context of the 3D Knowledge Model – that's how they know what is in and out of tolerance, established by policies resulting in the SOI.

IN:3-2 Model and assess the gap

This practice develops and uses gap assessment models to determine the scope, urgency, and impact of out-of-tolerance conditions between the current state and the organizational SOI to create, protect, and deliver digital business value.

APPENDIX B:
The Digital Value Capability Maturity Model

Appendix B: The Digital Value Capability Maturity Model

A capability maturity model provides a basis for an organization to gauge various organizational capabilities, and the maturity of management or the level of rigor the organization applies toward achieving and maintaining those capabilities.

We've adapted the US Department of Energy's Cybersecurity Capability Maturity Model (C2M2) (US Department of Energy, 2022) for use with the DVMS and the Z-X Model capabilities to create the DVCMM.

The DVMS represents the minimum viable capability the organization must demonstrate to create, protect, and deliver digital business value; the DVCMM has four levels (numbered 0 to 3). To meet those minimum capabilities, an adopting organization must achieve level 3 (the fourth level) to ensure the value created is appropriately protected.

The DVCMM (Table B.1) is an uncomplicated approach for determining the organizational capability to create, protect, and deliver digital business value. It's a binary evaluation: the organization either does something or doesn't; the outcomes and associated process maturity must be measurable, documented, and auditable.

Existing organizational policies establish the basis for execution. The organization measures process performance[42] to ensure that the Z-X Model capabilities fit its intended purpose and deliver digital business value that meets expectations.

Table B.1 The DVCMM

Level	Characteristics	Management	Artifacts
Level 0	There are no processes to perform the capability-related practice areas	None	None
Level 1	Processes to perform the capability-related practice areas are unplanned and informal	Ad hoc	Some processes are repeatable There is documentation for some processes There are measures and metrics for some processes There are policies that provide some (potentially incomplete) guidance governing establishing measures and metrics Existing measures and metrics provide the basis for action

Table continues

---

42   The Z-X Model capabilities do not extend to process; the model covers practice areas and practices that form the basis for areas of improvement. Processes execute the activities associated with one or more practices.

Table continued

Level	Characteristics	Management	Artifacts
Level 2	There is documentation for the processes that execute the capability-related practice areas Stakeholders are identified and involved There are adequate resources to support the process Use standards or guidelines to support the implementation of processes related to capabilities and practice areas	Structured	The organization adopts a structured approach to creating, protecting, and delivering digital business value The organization uses risk-based policies to create measures and metrics that express the organizational SOI There is a traceable link between business value and resource allocation to create, protect, and deliver The organization implements relevant processes to support the Z-X Model practice areas There is process documentation There are measures and metrics to determine that the processes are fit for use Auditable documentation shows stakeholder identification and their respective involvement with the appropriate processes Evidence shows the adopted standards have supporting adaptation documentation with the appropriate fit-for-use measures and metrics There are staff awareness and training plans to enable skilled and knowledgeable staff to support the Z-X Model practice areas and associated processes
Level 3	Governance and policies guide activities Policies include compliance requirements for specified standards or guidelines Activities are periodically reviewed for conformance to policy Responsibility and authority for each process are assigned Personnel performing the processes associated with practices and related capabilities have adequate skills and knowledge	Controlled	Measures and metrics are used to determine that the processes: • Are fit for purpose • Comply with relevant internal and external requirements • Assure strategic policy execution There is proof that stakeholders are identified, accountability is established, and responsibilities are detailed All Z-X Model-associated practice areas and the resulting processes are adequately staffed at the level required to create, protect, and deliver digital business value Policies and procedures are applied to periodically assess personal skills and knowledge, to ensure staff have and use the required skills and knowledge to create, protect, and deliver digital business value

B.1 DVCMM capabilities, characteristics, and management

The Z-X Model overlays existing capabilities and practices (grouped into the practice areas identified in section 6.1.3). Consequently, the characteristics of the model are intentionally broad; they represent the organizational capabilities necessary to achieve a given maturity level. The term "management" connotes the organizational level of rigor applied to the Z-X Model's practice-area-related processes.

Level 0

- **Capability** The organization lacks the necessary awareness and structure to consistently generate, secure, and provide digital business value. It also does not have any measures or metrics in place to ensure that policies are being executed effectively and that the digital solutions are fit for purpose
- **Characteristics** The organization does not discernibly have any of the capabilities of the Z-X Model, which indicates a lack of understanding of its use as an overlay to improve performance
- **Management** The organization does not know or understand the capabilities necessary to create, protect, and deliver digital business value, or to exhibit discernible or objectively measurable action.

Level 1

- **Capability** The organization performs processes that create, protect, and deliver digital business value at an ad-hoc level. Performance assessment might involve some measures and metrics. However, these measures and metrics don't provide meaningful insight leading to actionable information, because there are no overarching policies to establish performance goals and consistent behavior
- **Characteristics** The organization performs an initial set of associated Z-X Model practice-related processes that are unplanned or informal. There is little or no documentation used in the performance of these processes, and no assurance of repeatability
- **Management** The organization may perform some activities associated with Z-X Model practice areas, but only on an ad-hoc basis. There is no assurance of reliable or repeatable outcomes.

Level 2

- **Capability** The organization adopts a structured approach to creating, protecting, and delivering digital business value. It establishes risk-informed policies that drive strategies to develop measures and metrics that express the organizational SOI. Resource allocation is value-based. The organization has adopted and adapted the relevant Z-X Model practice areas to close identified performance gaps. The processes associated with each practice area support appropriate measurements and metrics to ensure they are fit for use
- **Characteristics** The organization documents Z-X Model practice-area-related processes based on established strategy-risk-informed policies and governance. It identifies and assigns accountable and responsible stakeholders for process performance, metrics, and outcomes. The organization provides adequate resources to implement Z-X Model practice-area-related processes
- **Management** The organization establishes a structured approach to creating, protecting, and delivering digital business value. Z-X Model practice-area-related process activities conform to process documentation. The stakeholders in the outcomes of these processes play an active role in those processes. The organization provides the necessary funding and resources to create, protect, and deliver digital business value consistent with the organizational SOI. The organization follows established standards, frameworks, and methods.

Level 3

- **Capability** The organization is "under control." Governance and strategy-risk-informed policies guide all activities. Z-X Model capabilities, internal needs, external requirements, and the dynamic threat landscape are part of the ongoing assessment, balanced against the organizational SOI. The organization identifies and assigns stakeholder accountability and responsibility. Part of accountability and responsibility is finding and closing gaps in Z-X Model capabilities, personnel skills, and value performance
- **Characteristics** All organizational DVMS-related activities are guided by policy and subject to oversight. The policies address internal needs and external requirements to establish a basis to respond to the dynamic threat landscape. The organization periodically reviews DVMS-related activities to ensure policy compliance. Personnel has assigned responsibility and authority for practices and conformance to policy
- **Management** The organization ensures the execution of strategic policies that are consistent with its SOI. It establishes a reporting scheme that identifies performance gaps and ensures that Z-X Model practice-area-related processes are fit for use, are fit for purpose, and deliver the desired digital business value.

B.2   DVCMM quality is (almost) free

Unprotected value contributes to higher costs. By separating the inseparable, creating value without appropriate protections, the organization elevates its exposure to cybersecurity risk and associated costs to respond to and recover from to a cybersecurity breach.[43] Why? How is this possible?

Consider the following analogy. You should take your car to your auto mechanic for preventative maintenance. Suppose you ignore changing the oil. You're likely to experience complete engine failure and a voided warranty and incur an expense of at least 10% of the car purchase price – to say nothing about aggravation, lost productivity, the cost of a rental car, and more. The decision to ignore recommended maintenance puts you in a self-insuring position against engine failure. Take incremental steps to "appropriately protect" the car value and avoid unnecessary engine replacement expenses.

With the incremental cost of performing regular oil changes for your car, even if you keep the car for ten years and change the oil and oil filter every quarter, the total cost for the oil changes will likely be less than 25% of the cost of replacing the engine.

The same is true for digital value. Combining value creation with value protection requires a relatively small incremental cost. The perspectives of the implementor and auditor must be represented on the solution development team. Ideally, fill the roles with different people. In a small organization with insufficient resources, one person must provide the two perspectives.

The DVCMM provides a roadmap supporting incremental improvements to create and protect digital business value for stakeholders.

---

43   It is also likely that it will pay higher premiums on cybersecurity insurance.

Glossary

Glossary

3D Knowledge Model™
A guide to handling knowledge management mentorship, based on three axes.

adapt
In the NIST Cybersecurity Framework, "adapt" refers to the management decisions that result from the strategic governance decisions to "adopt" a framework or cybersecurity informative reference.

adopt
In the NIST Cybersecurity Framework, "adopt" refers to the strategic governance decision to select and apply a framework or cybersecurity informative reference.

AICPA
American Institute of Certified Public Accountants.

ambidextrous
In the DVMS context, able to work both *on* and *in* the system simultaneously.

attack vector
The way, means, or approach a bad or threat actor uses to gain potentially illegal access to computer systems.

Bloom's taxonomy
A hierarchical set of verbs that describes learning objectives.
https://www.bloomstaxonomy.net/

capability
In the systems engineering sense, "capability" is defined as the ability to execute a specified course of action. We also use it to aggregate one or more practice areas.
https://en.wikipedia.org/wiki/Capability_(systems_engineering)

CAS
Complex adaptive system.

chaotic (Cynefin domain)
The domain of uncertainty lacks clarity regarding both cause and effect, requiring a new or innovative approach.

clear (Cynefin domain)
The domain where the situation is stable and there are known cause-and-effect relationships, enabling best-practice resolution.

CMS
Configuration management system – a set of tools and data used to collect, store, manage, update, analyze, and present data about all configuration items and their relationships.

complex (Cynefin domain)
The domain of uncertainty where it's difficult to determine cause and effect.

complicated (Cynefin domain)
The domain where situations are uncertain but not entirely unknown, with a range of possible resolutions.

confusion (Cynefin domain)

The domain where there is no clear application of the other domains.

control

We define a generic control as part of a process that ensures repeatability. In cybersecurity, the control supports the identification, detection, protection, response, and recovery from a cybersecurity incident. Think of controls as requirements to produce or enable an outcome.

COSO

Committee of Sponsoring Organizations of the Treadway Commission.

CPD Model

Create, protect, and deliver digital business value – the bottom layer of the DVMS, an abstraction or conceptualization of an organizational operating system.

CUI

Controlled Unclassified Information (CUI) – a category of unclassified information within the US Federal government. It is used extensively in NIST Special Publication (SP) 800-171.

culture

In an organization, culture is "the way we do things" based on the beliefs and attitudes that underlie the resulting behaviors.

CVE

Common Vulnerabilities and Exposures (CVE®) – a list of publicly disclosed cybersecurity vulnerabilities that is free to search, use, and incorporate into products and services. https://www.cve.org/

CVSS

The Common Vulnerability Scoring System (CVSS) – a free and open industry standard for assessing the severity of computer system security vulnerabilities. CVSS attempts to assign severity scores to vulnerabilities, allowing responders to prioritize responses and resources according to a threat. Scores are calculated based on a formula that depends on several metrics that approximate the ease of exploitation and its impact. Scores range from 0 to 10, with 10 being the most severe. While many utilize only the CVSS base score to determine severity, temporal and environmental scores also exist to factor in the availability of mitigations and how widespread vulnerable systems are within an organization.
https://en.wikipedia.org/wiki/Common_Vulnerability_Scoring_System

cybersecurity incident

If not addressed or resolved, a generic incident results in an unplanned negative impact on the business, including personal productivity. A cybersecurity incident is an incident with a cybersecurity origin.

DBRM

Digital business risk management.

DBRO

Digital business risk officer – the role of an individual who champions DBRM inherent in strategy-risk, ensuring these considerations are at the forefront of all decisions.

DFARS

The Defense Federal Acquisition Regulation Supplement provides uniform acquisition policies for the US Department of Defense.
https://www.acq.osd.mil/DPAP/dars/dfarspgi/current/index.html

DIB

The Defense Industrial Base lists those companies that do business with the US Department of Defense. It includes both prime contractors and their associated subcontractors.

double-loop learning

The use of experience to modify decision-making rules or goals. The first loop uses existing goals and rules; the second loop examines the outcomes against expectations and provides appropriate modification for improvement. This is a critical aspect of agile retrospectives.

DVCMM

Digital Value Capability Maturity Model – an adaptation of the US Department of Energy's Cybersecurity Capability Maturity Model (C2M2) for use with the DVMS and the Z-X Model capabilities.

DVMS

The Digital Value Management System® (DVMS) – the overarching system that delivers digital value to stakeholders. It is composed of three adaptable and scalable layers: the DVMS, the Z-X Model, and the CPD Model. The DVMS is a "black box" to the outside world. It overlays what the organization does and how it produces outcomes for stakeholders. The Z-X Model includes seven core organizational capabilities (Govern, Assure, Plan, Design, Change, Execute, and Innovate). The CPD Model operationalizes the Z-X Model.

DVMS FastTrack™

A structured approach to adapt the NIST-CSF and one or more of its informative references. It provides rapid adaptation, implementation, operation, and improvement of the relevant cybersecurity control families. FastTrack™ addresses adaptation following the strategic decision to adopt the NIST-CSF.

ERM

Enterprise risk management (ERM) in business includes the methods and processes used by organizations to manage risks and seize opportunities related to achieving their objectives.
https://en.wikipedia.org/wiki/Enterprise_risk_management

ERM framework

A framework for risk management. In this context, a framework describes what to do, not how to do it.

escalation archetype

Part of the visual language of systems thinking. The escalation archetype system can be described using causal loop diagrams that consist of balancing and reinforcing loops. https://en.wikipedia.org/wiki/Escalation_archetype

governance

The processes of interaction and decision-making among the actors involved in a collective problem that lead to the creation, reinforcement, or reproduction of social norms and institutions.
https://arcticyearbook.com/arctic-yearbook/2015/2015-preface

Governance/Assurance loop

The outer loop of the CPD Model. The "Governance" side turns organizational strategy into policies that are executed to create, protect, and deliver digital business value. The "Assurance" side assesses the performance of the organizational capabilities that execute the strategic policies, and whether the value created is appropriately protected.

Governance/Execution loop

One of the two main inner loops of the CPD Model. It turns policies into organizational capabilities that create, protect, and deliver digital business value, and measures the capability to execute strategic and operational intent to produce this value.

GQM

Goal, question, metric (GQM) – an established goal-oriented approach to software metrics to improve and measure software quality. https://en.wikipedia.org/wiki/GQM

GQM+Strategies

An adaptation of GQM, designed to ensure that the metrics reflect the relationship between development-goal-related activities and the business-level strategy.

hacktivist

A computer hacker with a social or political cause.

HIDS

A host-based intrusion detection system (HIDS) runs on an individual host or device on the network. A HIDS monitors the inbound and outbound packets from a device and only alerts the user or administrator if suspicious activity is detected. https://en.wikipedia.org/wiki/Intrusion_detection_system

informative reference (IR)

Informative references are citations of detailed cybersecurity documents to any combination of functions, categories, and subcategories within the NIST-CSF. They demonstrate how a given cybersecurity document can be used in coordination with the framework for cybersecurity risk management. https://www.nist.gov/cyberframework/informative-references

ISO/IEC 27000

The ISO/IEC 27000 series comprises information security standards published jointly by the International Organization for Standardization (ISO) and the International Electrotechnical Commission (IEC). https://en.wikipedia.org/wiki/ISO/IEC_27000-series

malware

A portmanteau of malicious software. It is intended to damage or disable computers and computer systems. https://en.wikipedia.org/wiki/Malware

misuse case

The term "misuse case" case is derived from and is the inverse of "use case." It refers to executing a malicious act *against* a system, while a use case is an action taken *by* the system. https://en.wikipedia.org/wiki/Misuse_case

model

An abstracted pattern of behaviors that supports understanding or replicating a set of processes, activities, or tasks.

MVC

Minimum viable capabilities.

NIDS

A network intrusion detection system (NIDS) is placed at a strategic point (or points) within the network to monitor traffic to and from all devices on the network. It performs an analysis of passing traffic on the entire subnet and matches the traffic that passes on the subnet to the library of known attacks. https://en.wikipedia.org/wiki/Intrusion_detection_system

NIST

The National Institute of Standards and Technology (NIST) – part of the US Department of Commerce, and one of the oldest physical science laboratories in the US. https://www.nist.gov/

NIST SP 800-171

The full title of this publication is *Protecting Controlled Unclassified Information in Nonfederal Systems and Organizations*. https://csrc.nist.gov/publications/detail/sp/800-171/rev-2/final

NIST SP 800-39

The full title of this publication is *Managing Information Security Risk: Organization, Mission, and Information System View* https://nvlpubs.nist.gov/nistpubs/Legacy/SP/nistspecialpublication800-39.pdf

NIST SP 800-53

The full title of this publication is *Security and Privacy Controls for Information Systems and Organizations*. https://csrc.nist.gov/publications/detail/sp/800-53/rev-5/final

PCI DSS

The Payment Card Industry Data Security Standard (PCI DSS) – an information security standard for organizations that handle branded credit cards from the major card schemes. The PCI DSS is mandated by the card brands but administered by the Payment Card Industry Security Standards Council. The Standard was created to increase controls around cardholder data, thereby reducing credit card fraud.

PDSA

Plan-Do-Study-Adjust (PDSA; also Plan-Do-Check-Act or PDCA) comes from the work of W. Edwards Deming; it is a systematic cycle for learning to continually improve a product, process, or service. PDSA is an updated version. https://deming.org/explore/pdsa/

phishing

The fraudulent attempt to obtain sensitive information or data, such as usernames, passwords, credit card details, or other sensitive details, by impersonating oneself as a trustworthy entity in digital communication. https://en.wikipedia.org/wiki/Phishing

PMO

A program or project management office (PMO) is responsible for defining and maintaining program or project management standards across an organization.

practice

Practices aggregate one or more processes that define or describe how an organization does things.

practice area

Groups of practices that describe what an organization does – not how it does it.

principle

An immutable proposition or value that is a guide for behavior or evaluation. https://en.wikipedia.org/wiki/Principle

process

A set of activities designed to accomplish an objective, with appropriate controls to ensure repeatability at producing the desired outcome.

program management

The process of managing several related projects.

project management

Projects introduce change. Project management is the process of leading the work of a team to achieve the project's goals and meet the success criteria at a specified time.
https://en.wikipedia.org/wiki/Project_management

QO–QM

Question Outcome–Question Metric (QO–QM) – an adaptation of the GQM+Strategies approach to fit the CPD Model. It starts by asking about the outcome to assure it aligns with the strategy-risk. Once it is aligned, the outcome becomes the goal for GQM.

ransomware

A type of malware that encrypts organizational data and systems until and unless a ransom is paid. The attackers may also threaten the victim with data exposure unless the ransom is paid – also known as "extortion."
https://en.wikipedia.org/wiki/Ransomware

risk appetite

The level of risk that an organization is prepared to accept before action is deemed necessary to reduce the risk.
https://en.wikipedia.org/wiki/Risk_appetite

risk management

The identification, evaluation, and prioritization of risks (defined in ISO 31000 as the effect of uncertainty on objectives), followed by the coordinated and economic application of resources to minimize, monitor, and control the probability or impact of unfortunate events or to maximize the realization of opportunities.
https://en.wikipedia.org/wiki/Risk_management

SOA

The statement of applicability (SOA) is one of the required documents for ISO 27001 compliance/certification. It lists all of the controls in Annex A and details whether they are included or excluded, with appropriate justification and information about their implementation.

SOI

Strategic and operational intent.

strategy

A strategy forms the basis for the choices that underlie the system that delivers value via the DVMS.

Strategy/Governance loop

One of the two main inner loops of the CPD Model. It turns strategy into policies that are adapted and executed via organizational capabilities, actions, and feedback; these may cause a realignment of policy or strategy.

strategy-risk

A single-entity concept, based on the authors' experience. We found that treating strategy and risk as separate concepts didn't work.

system

A group of interrelated and interacting parts that are organized to accomplish a purpose. A system is not the sum of its parts – it is the product of interactions between the parts.

ISO/IEC/IEEE defines a system as follows: "A complete system includes all of the associated equipment, facilities, material, computer programs, firmware, technical documentation, services, and personnel required for operations and support to the degree necessary for self-sufficient use in its intended environment."
https://www.iso.org/standard/81702.html

system archetype

System archetypes are patterns of behavior of a system. Systems expressed by circles of causality have, therefore, similar structures.
https://en.wikipedia.org/wiki/System_archetype

systems thinking

An approach that helps us understand complex situations by examining how different parts of a system interact and influence each other.

tension metrics

Metrics that attempt to balance three or more related and competing metrics.

threat actor

In computer security, a threat is a potential adverse action or event that has been facilitated by a vulnerability, resulting in an unwanted impact on a computer system or application. A threat actor is an entity that carries out this action.

threat landscape

A collection of threats in a particular domain or context, with information on identified vulnerable assets, threats, risks, threat actors, and observed trends.
https://itlaw.wikia.org/wiki/Threat_landscape

use case

A list of actions or event steps that defines the interactions between a role (or actor) and a system to achieve a goal.
https://en.wikipedia.org/wiki/Use_case

value

The perceived benefit of something. It is the customer or user who determines the value of something.

value stream

A series of activities that creates a flow of value to the customer (i.e., the product or service).

vishing

Otherwise known as "voice phishing" – a form of criminal phone fraud that uses social engineering via telephone to gain access to private personal and financial information for monetary gain.
https://en.wikipedia.org/wiki/Voice_phishing

VPN

A virtual private network (VPN) provides privacy, anonymity, and security to users by creating a private network across a public network.
https://en.wikipedia.org/wiki/Virtual_private_network

XaaS (something as a service)

A general term for cloud-based services, such as software as a service (SaaS) and platform as a service (PaaS).

Z-X Model

Part of the DVMS. It represents the high-level aspect of the DVMS that executes a strategy. The objective is to recognize and action a value gap. The Z-X Model includes a common set of capability flows across multiple DVMS adaptations. It defines seven organizational capabilities: Govern, Assure, Plan, Design, Change, Execute, and Innovate.

References

References

Basili, V. R., Caldiera, G., and Rombach, H. D. (n.d.), The Goal Question Metric approach. https://www.cs.umd.edu/users/mvz/handouts/gqm.pdf.

Basili, V., Heidrich, J., Lindvall, M., Münch, J., Regardie, M., Rombach, D., Seaman, C., and Trendowicz, A. (2007). GQM+Strategies: A comprehensive methodology for aligning business strategies with software measurement. https://doi.org/10.48550/arXiv.1402.0292.

Bixenspan, D. (2023). Whatever happened to Kodak? https://www.slashgear.com/1386360/whatever-happened-to-kodak-explained/.

Cunliff, E. (2018). Connecting systems thinking and action. *Systems Thinker*. https://thesystemsthinker.com/connecting-systems-thinking-and-action/.

Deloitte (2013). Exploring strategic risk: 300 executives around the world say their view of strategic risk is changing. https://www.deloitte.com/content/dam/assets-shared/legacy/docs/services/risk-advisory/2022/dttl-grc-exploring-strategic-risk.pdf.

Deming, W. E. (1982). *Out of the Crisis*. MIT Press, Cambridge, Massachusetts.

Dyer, J., Furr, N., Lefrandt, C., and Howell, T. (2023). Why innovation depends on intellectual honesty. https://sloanreview.mit.edu/article/why-innovation-depends-on-intellectual-honesty/.

Edmonds, S. C. (2014). *The Culture Engine: A Framework for Driving Results, Inspiring Your Employees, and Transforming Your Workplace*. Wiley, Hoboken, New Jersey.

Groysberg, B., Lee, J., Price, J., and Cheng, J. Y.-J. (2018). The leader's guide to corporate culture. *Harvard Business Review* (January–February). https://hbr.org/2018/01/the-leaders-guide-to-corporate-culture.

Hollister, R., Tecosky, K., Watkins, M., and Wolpert, C. (2021). Why every executive should be focusing on culture change now. https://sloanreview.mit.edu/article/why-every-executive-should-be-focusing-on-culture-change-now/.

Kim, D. (2018). Behavior over time diagrams: seeing dynamic interrelationships. https://thesystemsthinker.com/behavior-over-time-diagrams-seeing-dynamic-interrelationships/.

Kotter, J. P. (1995). Leading change: Why transformation efforts fail. *Harvard Business Review* (May–June). https://hbr.org/1995/05/leading-change-why-transformation-efforts-fail-2.

Kotter, J. P. (2012). *Leading Change*. Harvard Business Review Press, Boston, Massachusetts.

Meadows, D. (1999). Leverage points: Places to intervene in a system. https://www.donellameadows.org/wp-content/userfiles/Leverage_Points.pdf.

Milian, M. (2011). Steve Jobs fielded some customer service requests. https://edition.cnn.com/2011/11/22/tech/innovation/jobs-excerpt-customer-service/.

Mind Tools (2024). The Cynefin framework: Using the most appropriate problem-solving process. https://www.mindtools.com/atddimk/the-cynefin-framework.

Moskowitz, D. and Nichols, D. M. (2022). *A Practitioner's Guide to Adapting the NIST Cybersecurity Framework*. TSO, London.

Nadella, S. (2017). *Hit Refresh: The Quest to Rediscover Microsoft's Soul and Imagine a Better Future for Everyone*. Harper Business, New York.

Nevis, E. C., DiBella, A. J, and Gould, J. M. (1995). Understanding organizations as learning systems. https://sloanreview.mit.edu/article/understanding-organizations-as-learning-systems/.

Nicholson, J. (2021). Using positive reinforcement to influence the behavior of others. https://www.psychologytoday.com/gb/blog/persuasion-bias-and-choice/202106/using-positive-reinforcement-influence-the-behavior-others.

Pedler, M., Burgoyne, J., and Boydell, T. (1996). *The Learning Company. A Strategy for Sustainable Development.* McGraw Hill, London.

Perry, M. J. (2019). Only 52 US companies have been on the Fortune 500 since 1955, thanks to the creative destruction that fuels economic prosperity. https://www.aei.org/carpe-diem/only-52-us-companies-have-been-on-the-fortune-500-since-1955-thanks-to-the-creative-destruction-that-fuels-economic-prosperity/.

Rowley, J. (2007). The wisdom hierarchy: representations of the DIKW hierarchy. *Journal of Information and Communication Science* 33 (2): 163–180.

Senge, P. M. (2006). *The Fifth Discipline: The Art and Practice of the Learning Organization* (2nd edition). Currency, New York.

Senge, P., Kleiner, A., and Roth, G. (1999). *The Dance of Change: The challenges to sustaining momentum in a learning organization.* Doubleday, New York.

Snowden, D. J. and Boone, M. E. (2007). A leader's framework for decision making. https://hbr.org/2007/11/a-leaders-framework-for-decision-making.

Vector Solutions (2019). What is a learning organization? https://www.vectorsolutions.com/resources/blogs/what-is-a-learning-organization/.

US Department of Energy (2022). Cybersecurity Capability Maturity Model (C2M2). https://www.energy.gov/sites/default/files/2022-06/C2M2%20Version%202.1%20June%202022.pdf.

Watkins, K. E. and Marsick, V. J. (1992). Building the learning organisation: A new role for human resource developers. *Studies in Continuing Education* 14(2), 115–129. https://doi.org/10.1080/0158037920140203.

Westrum R. (2004). A typology of organisational cultures. *BMJ Quality & Safety* 3(Suppl 2), ii22–ii27. https://qualitysafety.bmj.com/content/13/suppl_2/ii22.info.

Whittington, R., Regner, P., Angwin, D., Johnson, G., and Scholes, K. (2020). *Exploring Strategy: Text and Cases* (12th edition). Pearson Education, Harlow.

Wikipedia (2024a). Cynefin framework. Last modified Apr. 02, 2024. https://en.wikipedia.org/wiki/Cynefin_framework.

Wikipedia (2024b). Double-loop learning. Last modified Dec. 29, 2023. https://en.wikipedia.org/wiki/Double-loop_learning.

Wikipedia (2024c). Escalation archetype. Last modified Oct. 17, 2023. https://en.wikipedia.org/wiki/Escalation_archetype.

Wikipedia (2024d). Likert scale. Last modified Mar. 07, 2024. https://en.wikipedia.org/wiki/Likert_scale.

Wikipedia (2024e). Mental model. Last modified Feb. 24, 2024. https://en.wikipedia.org/wiki/Mental_model.

Wikipedia (2024f). *The Day the Universe Changed.* Last modified Apr. 22, 2024. https://en.wikipedia.org/wiki/The_Day_the_Universe_Changed.

Index

Index